Cookin' Southern

Vegetarian Style

by

Ann Jackson

Book Publishing Company
Summertown, Tenn.

Cover design: Randa Abbas
Cover photo: Digital Imagery ® 1999 PhotoDisc, Inc.
Interior design: Warren C. Jefferson

Published in the United States by
Book Publishing Company
P.O. Box 99
Summertown, TN 38483
1-888-260-8458
www.bookpubco.com

ISBN 1-57067-092-7

Jackson, Ann
      Cookin' southern, vegetarian style / by AnnJackson
          p. cm.
      Includes index.
      ISBN 1-57067-092-7 (alk. paper)
      1. Vegetarian cookery. 2. Cookery, American--Southern style.
   TX837.J12 2000
   641.5'636'0975--dc21   99-462153

Contents

To my grandmothers,

With love as deep as their bowls.

Introduction

*The blue bowl stood there, seemingly full for-
ever, no matter how deeply or rapaciously we
dipped, as if it had no bottom. And she dipped
up soup, dipped up lima beans, dipped up
stew. Forked out potatoes. Spooned out rice
and peas and corn. And in the light and
warmth that was Her, we dined.*

Alice Walker
My Mother's Blue Bowl

When sitting down to write this book, I thought long and hard about what is Southern cooking. What is the one thing that you can point to and say, "Oh, yes, that's it, that is real Southern cooking." Is it a certain ingredient, a special utensil, or a particular cooking method? I asked both my grandmothers, who have lived and cooked in the South their whole lives. "Well, no one thing in particular," they said. I knew it was more than bacon grease, fatback, and over-cooked vegetables but what exactly, I couldn't put my finger on. Then one day, it came to me like a stroke of lightning. It's attitude, plain and simple.

It's kitchens in the summer and tomato sandwiches;

Slapping mosquitoes and swatting flies;

Tall sweating glasses of iced sweet tea with a sprig of fresh peppermint;

Rocking chairs and folded paper fans on the front porch;

Grits in the morning and cornbread at night;

Blackberry picking—chiggers, ticks, stickers, snakes, and all;

Poke salad and rocket (not arugula);

Kudzu, cotton fields, corn pones, and coon hounds.

It's mimosas, magnolias, gardenias, and pecans.

Sleeping at night with the windows open to the lullaby of bullfrogs, crickets, peepers, whippoorwill, and cicada;

It's a heaping plate of green beans with a couple of slices of onions and red tomatoes sliced into it;

Church suppers and bake sales, picnics at the creek;

Strawberry jam on a hot, split biscuit;

Muscadines and scuppernongs;

Names like Do-i, Ed Ray, Nell Vaughn, and Aunt Sukee;

Moon pies, fried apple pies, and Goo-Goo Clusters;

Black snakes, crawdads, and tadpoles.

It's hotter than a June Bride, pure as the driven snow, and country comes to town; Elvis and deep-fried banana and peanut butter sandwiches;

Johnny Cash and June Carter, Daniel Boone and Davy Crockett;

A president named Jimmy, not James;

A swimming hole, not a swimming pool;

It's I recon, I'm fixin', I'll swannee, and I'll be dad-gummed;

Good manners and gentleman callers;

Getting your newspaper, your live bait, and your Pepsi all at the same store.

It's poison ivy, spider webs, and tobacco spit;

Myrtle Beach to Memphis, Swannee to Shiloh;

Arrowheads and Civil war relics;

Afternoon teas, white gloves, and never wearing white shoes before Memorial Day;

It's watermelon, okra, and boiled peanuts;

Spanish moss, dilapidated barns, country roads, and Rock City;

Confederate jasmine, honeysuckle, church choirs, and white cornmeal;

A pack of peanuts poured in a bottle of Pepsi.

It's Tennessee Williams, William Faulkner, Truman Capote, and Eudora Welty;

Howard Finster, Ava Gardner, Bear Bryant, and bear footin';

It's red necks, red clay, and redeye gravy;

A Georgia peach, Tennessee tomato, Mississippi mud pie, and Florida crackers; Sweet white corn, molasses, apple butter, and deep-fried dill pickles;

It's sitting on the back porch listening to the grass grow;

Names like Unaka, Watauga, Waxahatchee, Saxapahaw, Tupelo, and Talahatchee;

Hammocks, hound dogs, and hoot owls;

Gumbo, corn dodgers, and bobwhites;

Deep woods, deep summer, and deep-dish apple pie, all washed down with an ice cold Blenheim's Extra Hot Ginger Ale.

It's knowing all these things, taking them deep into your heart, lying down on a bed covered with a chenille spread, resting your head on a feather pillow, and with a contented sigh saying, "I'm home."

7

So you want to cook Southern?

The following is a list of things you might want to have on hand.

1. *An apron:* I like to use a vintage floral pattern myself; a plain white butcher's apron will not do.

2. *Toasted sesame oil:* This is probably the most important ingredient as it duplicates the taste of salt pork, bacon grease, fatback, ham hock, pork rinds, or chitlins. Notice I did not say sesame oil; plain sesame oil will not do it. It must be toasted sesame oil or dark sesame oil. It's usually cheaper at an Oriental grocery store than at a natural foods store. This oil has a strong flavor. You won't want to use just sesame oil in a recipe— you'll only need anywhere from 1 teaspoon to a couple of tablespoons and can use a bland-tasting oil (such as canola) in the rest of the dish.

3. *White cornmeal:* It might not seem like the color of your cornmeal would make that much of a difference, but it is huge. People in the South don't eat yellow corn; we feed it to cows and horses. Cornbread made from yellow cornmeal will not taste the same or look the same than when you use white cornmeal. You'll have to put in sugar, and then you'll have Yankee cornbread.

4. *A timer*: I suppose you could cook Southern and not have a timer, but how would you ever keep from burning the rice?

5. *An electric skillet:* I know, I know, it doesn't make sense. I used to be a die-hard cook who believed you must have a flame to cook. Do you know how many times I've said, "Cooking with electricity is like cooking on a coat hanger"?

When we moved to the country, my dream came true. I was finally able to get me a gas stove. We had to order it, and it was six weeks before we got it. In the meantime, we got an electric skillet to do in a pinch. I can't tell you how good the "fried chicken" tofu was that came out of that electric skillet. At first I just couldn't understand it. Then, after careful observation, I figured it out. The electric skillet has some kind of temperature gauge that keeps stuff from burning. With a cast-iron skillet, you have to watch the tofu or it will surely burn. In an electric skillet, you can actually forget about it for up to 45 minutes or even an hour and a half, and the tofu just keeps getting crispier and yummier. (My brother once forgot his for five hours and said it was more like bacon than bacon.) It cooks more slowly so it has lots of time to soak up flavors and get that crispy skin-like texture on the outside.

When you cook meat, the animal fat gives it its flavor. When you cook tofu or seitan, you have to start from scratch to make it taste like something; so often-times, the longer it can cook, the more of a chance there is it will taste good.

PS: I still think microwaves are evil.

6. *Cast-iron skillet:* After singing the praises of the electric skillet, let's get down to brass tacks and talk about the real thing: the cast-iron skillet. Except for tofu, I use my cast-iron skillet for just about everything else that gets fried or sautéed. Nothing else will do for really good cornbread, and I have a special pan that I use only for pineapple upside-down cake.

Along with a good mixing bowl, your cast-iron skillet can help you connect to the apron strings of all the good cooks who have come along before you. Just seeing it sitting on your stove will give you confidence in your cooking and confidence in yourself. It is also the first thing I grab when I hear a spooky noise. When my husband is out of town, I take the skillet with me when I make the rounds and sleep with it beside me all night. It is my friend and protector.

Jack Butler, cook, writer, and Southern Renaissance man says, "Your cast-iron skillet should be roughly as old as you are." When Granny was moving from the house she had lived in for 93 years and she asked me what I wanted, the two things I wanted most were her cast-iron skillet, which belonged to her mother, and her glass refrigerator dishes. Get a good cast-iron skillet and season it well, (see the household hints on p.184) and you will have a friend for life.

7. *Good-tasting nutritional yeast:* I believe this is sold under the brand name Red Star Vegetarian Support Formula, but you don't usually see it sold as that in natural foods stores. It will usually just say yeast flakes or something like that. Once someone said to me, "Why do you say good-tasting nutritional yeast? Is there a bad-tasting one?" Well, actually, there is a horrible-tasting one: brewers yeast. Another time someone told me they tried to make "fried chicken" tofu, and it was awful. Upon questioning them thoroughly, I found they had used baking yeast!! There seems to be all sorts of

things at the natural foods store with the word "yeast" on it. Ask a clerk and use the words "yeast flakes"; that usually helps. So, it's not baking yeast, brewer's yeast, or any type of yeast protein powder, but Red Star yeast flakes.

8. *Tamari:* I had to look up the definition of this, as I always call tamari fancy soy sauce. Basically, that is what it is, an aged soy sauce made from soybeans, salt, and water. It is good to drizzle over things toward the end of cooking, as it will give a "browned" flavor to tofu, tempeh, or seitan.

9. *When I say butter:* I use soy margarine, olive oil, and toasted sesame oil exclusively. I know there are all kinds of oils from canola to walnut, but I'm in a rut when it comes to "grease." When I say butter, it is no more than a generic term for "grease" to me.

I'm just old fashioned. I still say "filling station" and am forever embarrassing myself by calling CDs "albums." If I've just spent any time around my grandmothers, I'll say "ice box," and I still say butter when I mean soy margarine. Recipes just don't sound the same to me when I say, "Cream sugar and soy margarine" or "cut in soy margarine." I have tried to remember to say soy margarine

in all the appropriate recipes, but if you see that I have forgotten somewhere, please excuse me. I'm still lost back somewhere in 1958.

10. *When I say mayonnaise:* I don't think it will matter in these recipes if you use tofu mayonnaise, eggless mayonnaise, or Duke's All-Purpose; just use your favorite.

11. *When I say soymilk:* I just about always use regular old non-fat soymilk. If you like rice milk better, that is fine, the recipes still work. The recipes will work even if you want to use real milk, but baking is a great way to try soymilk if you aren't sure you'll like it. It doesn't change the flavor of the food you're baking, and it works just the same.

12. *When I say vinegar:* I get into one vinegar and just stay in that rut until I try another one I really like. I can stay in the same vinegar rut for years. I went through rice vinegar, black Chinese vinegar, and now I'm in the balsamic vinegar stage. I suggest trying all kinds and getting into a groove with new vinegars.

13. *When I say tofu:* I usually just use a 1-pound block of tofu, and I like the firm, low-fat tofu you can buy these days.

14. *Miso:* This is fermented soybean paste. That may not sound appetizing, but miso is really good. There are all different flavors and colors. You should try them all and always have a couple kinds in your refrigerator. Something about miso always reminds me of country ham. (Spread it on tofu and put it under the broiler.) Miso soup is as easy as pouring hot water over a spoonful of miso in a coffee cup. There is nothing that can bring you around when you are just not feeling yourself like miso can. I have started using lighter-colored misos; they are milder. Light miso spread on toast with soy margarine is a favorite of mine.

Miso has a live bacteria like yogurt, so don't ever add it to something that's boiling. Just to end on a dramatic note, miso is what helped many of the Japanese survivors of the atomic bomb attacks of World War II reduce the effects of radiation sickness. It helps your body discharge radiation.

15. *Seitan, wheat meat, or gluten:* It is the protein from wheat, free of starch and bran. For more on seitan, see pages 138-39.

16. *Umeboshi plums:* These are small Japanese salted plums. They are great to use in place of a piece of salt pork, added after cooking any dried beans or green beans or when making soup or stew. I always fish the pit out of the plum and suck on it for a while; it feels very medicinal to me.

17. *What About Eggs? Using Egg Replacer*

Here is a good recipe for egg replacer that you can make at home. I make a full jar, and it seems to last a long time. This will work in just about any recipe that calls for egg replacer in this book.

Just mix equal parts of arrowroot flour and potato flour. I usually use about ½ cup of each, then mix it really well and keep it airtight in the fridge. When you want to use it, mix 1 tablespoon with 2 tablespoons water—that equals one egg. There are also several egg replacers on the market right now, all of them pretty good.

Another good egg replacer is 3 tablespoons of ground flaxseed combined with ½ cup cold water. This equals 2 large eggs. You can use a dry blender or a coffee or herb grinder to pulverize the flaxseeds.

18. *Dulse:* This is a seaweed that has been eaten for centuries by people of many cultures who live by the sea: the Irish, Newfoundlanders, and the like.

Not only is it rich in minerals, it's a great substitute for salt pork, that indispensible ingredient in any Southern recipe that calls for greens and/or beans.

19. *Chick-Pea Flour:* This is something you'd normally find in a recipe for Indian food, but I've commandeered it for duty in some of my gravy recipes, where it contributes a richness and body that plain white flour just won't give.

Salads

A smiling face is half the meal.

Latvian proverb

*The camellia buds are swelling and salvation
is at hand.*

George Wright

*Let first the onion flourish there,
Rose among the roots, the maiden-fair
Wine scented and poetic soul
of the capacious salad bowl.*

Robert Louis Stevenson

Scalded Salad for Four

Yield: 4 servings

This is a classic old-time Southern salad usually made with bacon fat. I use toasted (or dark) sesame oil.

Salad greens—spinach, arugula, or red or
   green leaf lettuce will work fine
½ carrot, grated
4 slices vegetarian bacon, or ½ cup roasted
   pecans or sesame seeds
½ cup olive oil
½ red onion, sliced into rings
2 tablespoons toasted sesame oil
1 tablespoon Dijon mustard
3 to 4 tablespoons balsamic vinegar

Arrange the greens in a salad bowl, and toss with the grated carrot. Cook the vegetarian bacon slices in a little of the olive oil in a skillet, then crumble over the salad.

Without cleaning out the skillet, add a little more olive oil and sauté the onion rings. Make a dressing by mixing the remaining olive oil, the sesame oil, mustard, and vinegar. When the onions are just limp, add this dressing to the skillet. Heat just a few minutes until all the ingredients are warmed through. Pour over the salad greens, and toss.

Addicting Tempeh "Chicken" Salad

Yield: 4 to 6 servings *(or 2 for tempeh addicts who can't even wait until it cools to eat it)*

I wasn't particularly tempted by the idea of steamed tempeh at first, but then I tried it. When I call this addicting, I'm not kidding. It is completely delicious. It's good in avocados, tomatoes, sandwiches, and more. I have made this and eaten the whole thing before it even got to the fridge. It's also good in tacos or burritos or as a chip dip. Please try this one.

One 8-ounce package tempeh
½ to ¾ cup mayonnaise
½ large onion, half grated and half chopped
   (or a few green onions)
½ cup finely chopped celery, including
   leaves, or 1 teaspoon celery seed
2 to 3 tablespoons good-tasting nutritional
   yeast flakes
½ teaspoon salt
Grated black pepper, to taste
Chopped tomatoes *(optional)*

Steam the tempeh lightly for about 25 minutes. Chop into chunks and put into a bowl with the rest of the ingredients. Grate as much of the onion as you can, and when it gets to your eyes badly, chop the rest. Refrigerate and serve when chilled.

14

Tommy Toe Salad

Yield: 4 to 6 servings

My Aunt Elsie is 89 years old and still has a garden bigger than any I would ever attempt. She doesn't just grow a few tomatoes and peppers. She will put out 50 tomatoes, corn, peas, beans, peppers, eggplant, and squash. Just the thought of keeping up with the weeding can give me a sinking spell, but Elsie chomps at the bit all winter to get her hands out in the dirt. She still lives on the same farm her father built and worked (now surrounded by K-Marts and shopping malls) and loves to walk around the yard with you and show you the flowers and shrubs that her mother planted back in the late 1800s.

One of my favorite things about Aunt Elsie's is her yellow and red tommy toe cherry tomatoes; they volunteer all over her garden. She says she has never planted them, they just come back wild year after year. It is obviously an heirloom seed and the best, sweetest, juiciest tomatoes ever. She saved me some seeds, and now they are one of the proudest fruits in my garden.

Besides tasting amazing popped into your mouth right off the vine, they are a great side dish. Kids think they are a special tomato just their size. Tommy toes make wonderful traveling food. You can have the taste of tomato without the soggy bread. Here's a good salad for tommy toes.

About 2 cups yellow, red, or mixed tommy
toes *(cherry tomatoes)*
1 red onion, thinly sliced
4 ears corn, cooked and cut off the cob
10 black olives *(optional)*
1 green pepper, finely chopped
½ cup chopped parsley
⅓ cup of your favorite salad dressing
Good-sized pinch salt and pepper *(if
using olives, watch the salt as
olives can be salty)*

Cut the tommy toes in half. Add the rest of the ingredients, and cover with dressing. Toss and let sit 5 minutes before serving.

Potato Salad

Yield: 8 to 10 servings

This salad is so good; lots of people tell me it's the best they've ever had. At potlucks or covered dish suppers, a crowd tends to form around the potato salad, and you hear exclamations of, "Why, homemade potato salad. I haven't had that in years!"

The secret of this salad is to mix it while the potatoes are hot and then let it sit awhile in the refrigerator.

5 to 6 large potatoes *(red skinned are best)*
1 onion
3 to 4 stalks celery with leaves, chopped
¼ teaspoon garlic powder
1 scant teaspoon dillweed
Salt and pepper, to taste*
2 tablespoons of the juice poured off the
　　top of a jar of pickles
½ to 1 cup mayonnaise *(if you eat dairy
　　products, put in an equal amount of
　　sour cream)*
¼ teaspoon turmeric (optional)
¼ teaspoon chopped parsley
1 to 2 tablespoons Dijon mustard
1 tablespoon poppy seeds
2 to 3 hard-boiled eggs, chopped *(optional)*

Crab Ralph

Yield: 4 servings as a salad,
6 servings as a sandwich filling

This recipe was discovered by accident when Lindsey spaced out and left three pallets of mushrooms outside overnight. We sold most of them off for cheap. I made stuffed mushrooms, cream of mushroom soup, and this wild salad of marinated mushrooms, artichoke hearts, and red onion rings, but there were still a lot of mushrooms left that were beginning to get those funky brown spots. So, Ralph, a true produce man at heart who lives by the motto "Sell it or smell it," offered to give this recipe a try. (I know this sounds weird, but Crab Ralph tastes best when the mushrooms are like this, one day from being thrown away.) We all loved what he made and thought it tasted like crab. Here's what he did.

2 to 3 cups very ripe whole mushrooms, finely chopped
2 tablespoons mayonnaise or sour cream substitute
½ tablespoon kelp powder
½ tablespoon Dijon mustard
½ tablespoon poppy seeds
Juice of ½ lemon
½ small onion, grated or finely chopped
½ cup chopped celery
Salt and pepper, to taste
Pinch of Old Bay Seasoning *(optional)*

Combine all the ingredients in a big bowl. Add more mayonnaise if you need to to make it moist, and adjust the seasonings to your liking. Serve immediately. This is best stuffed into avocados or tomatoes, or even on dark bread with tall glasses of Bloody Marys (or a spicy tomato juice for non-drinkers).

The Best Marinated Salad

Use 3 or more of the following ingredients—don't feel like you must use them all. The beauty of this salad is that it's just as good with a few items as with a lot. And it's so easy to throw together.

Layer in a large salad bowl in any order:
Alfalfa sprouts
Artichoke hearts
Asparagus tips
Avocados, chopped
Corn, cut off the cob
Cucumbers, peeled and sliced
Feta or blue cheese, cubed or crumbled
Green onions
Mushrooms, sliced
Olives, black or green
Parsley, finely chopped
Pimentos or red peppers
Red onions, sliced in rings
Tempeh, steamed and cubed

Tomatoes *(add just before serving—they'll get soggy otherwise)*

Now add the dressing. Almost any oil and lemon or vinegar dressing will do. Here's a good one that makes enough for about 10 to 12 servings.

⅔ cup olive oil
⅓ cup lemon juice, rice vinegar, or balsamic vinegar
1 teaspoon dry mustard, or 2 teaspoons Dijon mustard
2 cloves garlic, smashed
1 tablespoon fresh basil or oregano (½ teaspoon dried)
Salt and pepper, to taste

Mix well, then pour over the top of your layered salad. Barely toss and put in the refrigerator for a few hours. Before serving, toss again.

Tofu Egg Salad

Yield: 4 to 6 servings

This is sometimes called imitation egg salad. When you make it, grate as much of the onion as you can, until your eyes start to water unbearably. Then just chop the rest. If you have any pickles in the fridge, pour off a teaspoon of the juice into the salad. This should about do it.

1 pound tofu
1 stalk celery, finely chopped
½ onion, some grated and some chopped
1 tablespoon good-tasting nutritional
  yeast flakes
1 teaspoon poppy seeds
1 teaspoon Dijon mustard
¼ teaspoon dillweed
¼ cup mayonnaise
½ teaspoon turmeric *(optional—only if you
  want a yellow salad)*
Salt and pepper, to taste

Mash the tofu in a bowl. Add the rest of the ingredients, adding the turmeric a little at a time until the salad is the color you like; mix well.

Cole Slaw

Yield: 6 to 8 servings

Is there anything easier than cole slaw? Or better tasting? It's the perfect bite to take after a hot, buttery hushpuppy. Cool, sweet, and crunchy . . . what else could sit on a plate of barbecue and fit in so well? I never went to a backyard picnic that did not have cole slaw. Here's how I do it.

1 medium head cabbage
½ to ¾ cup mayonnaise
1 teaspoon poppy seeds
Juice of ½ lemon
Plenty of salt and black pepper
Pinch of sugar
½ small onion, grated *(optional)*
1 small carrot, grated *(optional)*

Slice the cabbage finely. This is very important. Make sure you slice the cabbage as thinly as possible, almost like shredding it.

Mix the other ingredients together in a measuring cup, pour over the cabbage, and toss. Cover and keep in the fridge for about an hour or until ready to eat.

A Mess of Tomatoes

Yield: 4 to 5 servings

Don't ever forget this as a great side dish in the summertime. You'll need:

3 to 4 big, ripe tomatoes—*different colored ones are great. (If you don't grow tomatoes and have the space to do it, you should.)*
1 big, old, pretty platter. *If you don't have one, use a glass pie plate. (If you don't have one, you need to go to more flea markets and get better kitchen stuff.)*
Salt, to taste

Peel and slice the tomatoes onto the platter until completely full; sprinkle with salt. Pass around as a side dish.

To make it a little more of a meal, spread thinly sliced red onions over the tomatoes, then drizzle with your favorite salad dressing. Top with 2 to 4 slices vegetarian bacon.

Tofu Mayonnaise or Sour Cream

Yield: 1½ cups

Egg-free! And a delicious alternative to dairy products.

½ pound tofu *(soft works best)*
3 tablespoons oil
Juice of ½ lemon
Salt and pepper, to taste

Combine all the ingredients in a blender, and mix until smooth. Stir in chopped pimentos if you like.

East Tennessee Favorites

But a dream should come true
and a heart should be filled,
and life should be lived
in the piney wood hills.

Buffy St. Marie

I'm doin' the best I can, with what I've got,
where I'm at, daily.

Hillbilly front porch philosophy

The violets in the mountains have broken the rocks.

Tennessee Williams

Greens

Yield: 3 to 5 large servings

So, you're ready to cook you up a mess of greens. What is a mess? I call it however much you can fit into the pot. Serve these with cornbread on the side.

1 bunch greens *(collard, kale, chard, turnip greens, beet greens, mustard greens, or your favorite)*
1 small dried hot pepper *(optional)*
2 to 3 tablespoons tamari
Juice of 1 lemon, or 3 tablespoons rice vinegar or hot pepper vinegar
Salt and pepper, to taste
1 to 2 teaspoons oil, if using an electric skillet *(toasted sesame is best)*

Cut the stems off the greens, and wash the leaves really well. You don't want them to be gritty. Don't worry about draining the wet leaves. Put the greens on a chopping board, and cut them lengthwise a couple of times, then cut across them about every 2 inches. (Many Southerners will swear that you have to tear the greens.)

Put about 3 cups water in a pot, and let it come to a boil. Put the greens into the pot; you may have to do this in batches as the greens will take up a lot of room until they cook down. Don't be shy; smash them down with a big spoon if you have to to get them in. You can also put in a smallish dried pepper pod if you have it. Cover and simmer about 45 minutes to 2 hours, depending on how you like your greens and what kind of greens you are using. If you are using kale, chard, or beet greens, they won't take as long to cook. Turnip greens, mustard greens, and collards (the king of greens) can take up to 2 hours to get that melt-in-your-mouth tenderness. Halfway through cooking, add ½ to 1 cup water with about 2 to 3 tablespoons tamari. You may want to toss the greens a couple of times during cooking.

The juice that is leftover from cooking is called "potlikker" and is a true delicacy. Heap the collards in a serving bowl, and drizzle lemon juice or vinegar over the top. Two or 3 pieces of cornbread are a must to use for sopping up the potlikker.

Greens are another good thing to cook in an electric skillet. You begin as above. Start out with any combination of olive and toasted sesame oil to make about 2 tablespoons Add greens to the skillet in batches if you need to. (The skillets usually have real tall lids.) Pour in about 2 cups water with about 2 to 3 tablespoons tamari. Cover and cook at about 300°F. You'll have to check this every 10 minutes or so to make sure the water has not cooked away. After about 15 minutes, turn down the heat to about 225°F. If you need to add more water, just add more, but you shouldn't need any more tamari. The greens will usually cook in 45 minutes; it all depends on the kind of green you use and your own taste. I like my greens melt-in-your-mouth. Every time I make greens like this, my husband says they're the best greens I ever made.

A small handful of chopped dried dulse (a seaweed) is good to add during the first 10 minutes or so of cooking. You don't have to do this, but dulse gives it that salt pork taste. Chinese black vinegar or balsamic vinegar is also very good on greens.

Greens and Peanut Sauce

Yield: 5 to 6 servings

I thought I had discovered something new one day when I put peanut sauce on my greens. Gooey was with me and said, "Big deal, people have been doing that in Africa forever." Why is that Southern? Because many things African have become inherent to southern American culture. Imagine the thrill of a homesick African cook upon finding that peanuts had become a major crop in the South, having come there from Africa. It was the chance to cook up a little bit of home, a mess of greens, peanut sauce, and a hot pepper. These are the roots of soul food.

1 bunch greens, cooked according to
    directions on the facing page

Sauce:
⅓ cup peanut butter
2 tablespoons toasted sesame oil
3 tablespoons rice vinegar or Chinese
    black vinegar
2 tablespoons tamari
¼ teaspoon cayenne
1 teaspoon sugar
l large clove garlic
Juice of 1 lime *(optional)*

Put all the sauce ingredients in a blender, and process until smooth. Enjoy over hot cooked greens.

Greens and Dumplings

Yield: 5 to 6 servings

1 pound *(or a good mess)* of greens
3 cups water
2 tablespoons tamari

Dumplings:
⅓ cup flour
⅔ cup white cornmeal
½ teaspoon salt
2 teaspoons baking powder
1 tablespoon toasted sesame oil
¼ cup soymilk *(more if needed)*

Prepare the greens for cooking (see Greens, p. 22). Put the greens, water, and tamari into a pot, bring to a boil, and simmer for 35 minutes to 1 hour, or until not quite done. I usually do this in an electric skillet. If you don't have one, use a pot with a tight-fitting lid.

While the greens are cooking, prepare the dumpling batter. Put all the dry ingredients into a bowl, and barely mix in the sesame oil with a fork. Next add the soymilk; the dough should be wet and firm but not runny. If you need to add more milk, do so a few drops at a time. The dough should be the consistency of modeling clay.

There should be plenty of water in the skillet from cooking the greens. If not, add more to barely cover the greens. Gently drop the batter by tablespoonfuls into the broth, leaving about ¼ inch between each dumpling. Cover and let steam over low heat for 20 minutes. Do not lift the lid.

Put the dumplings, greens, and broth into a bowl, and enjoy.

Aunt Sukie's Collard Greens

Yield: 3 servings

If you ever tasted country ham, the dulse will remind you of the intense saltiness of salt pork, so highly recommended by Southerners for cooking in a pot of greens.

2 tablespoons toasted sesame oil
1 onion, chopped *(optional)*
½ pound tofu, cubed *(strictly optional, if you're very hungry)*
2 tablespoons tamari
½ cup dulse, loosely packed and coarsely chopped
1 bunch leftover or partially cooked collards or favorite greens
Lemon juice, rice vinegar, Chinese black vinegar, or balsamic vinegar

Heat the oil in a cast-iron skillet. Add the onions, tofu, and tamari. Sauté until the onions are soft and the tofu is browned. Put in the dulse and let it all cook a few minutes. Add the cold greens, and barely toss, then cover. This is done when heated through.

Served with cornbread or pones to dip in the potlikker, this is unbeatable.

Fried Okra

Yield: 4 servings

Leftover boiled or steamed okra works fine in this recipe too, especially if you messed up and the okra got overcooked and slimy.

1 to 2 pounds okra
½ to 1 cup white cornmeal
1 to 2 teaspoons garlic powder
½ teaspoon each salt and pepper
½ cup toasted sesame oil

Rinse the okra and cut it in half lengthwise, leaving the stem ends on. Put the cornmeal, garlic powder, salt, and pepper into a paper bag, then add the okra and shake well. Heat the oil in a big skillet, and add the okra. Don't heap the okra in the skillet, just make a couple of batches. You want this to get crispy, not soggy. Don't stir this a lot, rather, turn it with a spatula.

To eat, drizzle a little tamari over the okra. When you eat these, pick them up by the nubby stem end, bite all the way down to the base, and discard the stem.

Succotash

Yield: 6 to 8 servings

There is no better summertime eating than succotash. Come the end of July or first of August, corn gets to be twelve ears for a dollar. In the South you can't go two feet without someone offering you large bags of tomatoes from "the garden." If you are pressed for time and absolutely have to, you can substitute canned whole tomatoes in this recipe, but nothing can take the place of fresh corn and okra.

Some people put lima beans in their succotash; in East Tennessee we never did. This is a must-have at a backyard picnic. It can be combined the day before and kept in the fridge until it's time to cook it.

4 ears fresh corn
5 vine-ripened tomatoes
½ pound okra *(about 3 to 4 cups chopped)*
Bread crumbs *(optional)*
Salt, pepper, and soy margarine, to taste

Cut the corn off the cob, and set aside. Skin the tomatoes by dropping them in boiling water for 15 seconds, then running under cold water; the skins will slip right off. Chop up and add to the corn. Trim off and discard the ends of the okra, then chop. Put the okra pieces in a saucepan, barely cover with water, and bring to a boil for about 2 minutes. Drain in a colander.

Preheat the oven to 350°F. Combine the okra with the corn and tomatoes, and salt generously. Add pepper, pour into a 9 x 13-inch casserole dish, and dust with bread crumbs, if using. Then dot the top generously with margarine. Bake for 1 hour in a deep dish, 45 minutes in a shallow one.

Great Smoky Mountains Green Beans

Yield: 5 to 6 servings

I will never forget the first time I had green beans after I left home. I was having dinner with my older cousin from New York. She put a big helping of beans on my plate and passed it to me.

"Excuse me," I said, "My beans haven't been cooked yet." I handed my plate back to her.

"What do you mean, I just took them off the stove myself."

"Well, they are warm," I said, "but they're still crunchy."

"Of course they're crunchy," she said horrified, "You don't want to overcook them."

It was then that it dawned on me how the rest of the world ate green beans. What? Cooked less than three hours? No ham bone? Still crunchy?

I've never had beans cooked exactly like this recipe (not even in other parts of the South). Here is the recipe I have come up with, sans ham bone.

3 to 4 pounds fresh string beans
½ teaspoon dry mustard
2 to 3 teaspoons toasted sesame oil
2 garlic cloves
1 tablespoon dark miso
1 to 2 umeboshi plums *(optional)*

To string the beans, snap off one end with your finger and pull it down the length of the bean. Do this to both ends. Now you won't have any tough strings when you eat the beans.

Rinse the beans well, put into a large pot, and cover with water. Bring to a boil and let cook a few minutes. Turn down the heat and simmer for about 4 hours or so. As they finish cooking, the beans should be dark green. At the end of the cooking time, dip out some of the hot water into a cup, dissolve the miso into it, and stir into the beans. When you serve them, put several slices of tomato and raw onion on top, and slice into the beans. Eat this all together. This is truly delicious. Don't worry about overcooking these; they can cook for 5 or 6 hours and keep getting better and better.

Black-Eyed Peas and "Fatback" (Hoppin John)

Yield: 8 to 10 servings

I was brought up to believe that a pot of beans was simply not edible if it didn't have some type of meat cooked with it. I fiddled around until I came up with something that brings out the taste of the beans just like I remember. If you can't find Pick-a-Peppa sauce in your store, you may substitute vegetarian Worcestershire, A-1 Sauce, White Tiger Sauce, or Perkin's Steak Sauce, but Pick-a-Peppa works best. Look for parrots on the label.

¼ cup tamari mixed with ¼ cup water

2 teaspoons dry mustard

2 teaspoons Pick-a-Peppa Sauce

1 to 2 cloves garlic

2 teaspoons toasted sesame oil

1 pound firm tofu

2 to 3 cups black-eyed peas, washed and picked through

1 white onion, chopped

2 teaspoons ketchup *(optional)*

½ teaspoon dried savory

1 teaspoon salt

Make a vegetarian "fatback" by stirring together the tamari, mustard, Pick-a-Peppa, garlic, and toasted sesame oil to make a marinade. Cut the tofu into chunks, and toss gently with the marinade. The longer this soaks, the better it is, but if you don't have much time, about an hour should do it.

Put the black-eyed peas in a pot with enough water to cover them, bring to a boil, and add the onion, ketchup, and savory. Turn down the heat and let simmer for about 45 minutes. When the peas are half done, add the tofu and the rest of the marinade, the salt, and pepper. Continue simmering and stir gently until the peas are soft. Serve this with hush-puppies or cornbread, collard greens, and boiled potatoes for good luck on New Year's Day.

"Fried Chicken" Tofu and Gravy

Yield: 3 servings *(with NO leftovers!)*

My sister Susan made up this recipe. I have never served this to anyone who did not love it, or say, "I can't believe it, . . . this tastes just like fried chicken." It is not only one of my favorites, but I could eat it for breakfast, lunch, and dinner. I also make this tofu in small cubes and have it in burritos or tortillas. It's great that way. It also tastes even better if it's leftover. Try to make enough to put some back (that's "save" to you Yankees) for the next day. This isn't easy though; however much I make, we always eat it all.

This is really easy to make, and there are as many ways to make it as there are kitchens. Susan likes to let hers cook covered for a long time and get really juicy. I like mine crispy and greasy. I really encourage you to try this one. Here's the way I do it:

Enough olive oil to cover the bottom
    of your skillet
2 to 3 tablespoons sesame seeds
1 pound tofu, sliced
½ cup good-tasting nutritional yeast flakes
2 tablespoons tamari

Heat the oil in a skillet. (I think an electric skillet works best, with the temperature set at about 300°F.) Add the sesame seeds. While these are heating, dredge each slice of tofu in the nutritional yeast until both sides are generously coated. When the seeds start to sizzle, arrange the tofu in the skillet. Drizzle the tamari over the top. Turn the slices and fry on both sides until crispy and brown. This can take anywhere from 15 minutes to 1 hour depending on how you like it. (I've cooked mine up to 2 hours.)

Gravy from "Fried Chicken" Tofu

Yield: 1 to 2 cups *(depending on how thick you want your gravy to be)*

Don't leave the drippings in your pan! Make gravy today! Enjoy over potatoes, rice, biscuits, stuffing, or whatever you're craving.

2 tablespoons soy margarine
Big handful flour *(O.K., about ⅓ cup)*
Any leftover nutritional yeast from "Fried Chicken" Tofu, p. 29
1 to 2 cups soymilk,* milk, or water *(Milk makes a very thick, rich gravy, but soymilk works just as well.)*
Salt, pepper, and tamari to taste

Leave the skillet just as it is from making the "Fried Chicken" Tofu. Add the margarine and let it melt. Stir in the flour and yeast until mixed, and let brown a little (but not burn) on medium-low heat. Add your liquid and continue stirring until thickened. Add salt, pepper, and tamari to taste.

* Be sure not to use sweetened soymilk, or you'll have dessert gravy!

Fried Green Tomatoes and Gravy

Yield: 4 servings

These tomatoes are good with real down-home dinners of beans and potatoes, or for breakfast with tofu scrambled eggs, potatoes, and biscuits.

4 tablespoons oil *(or enough to barely cover the bottom of the skillet)*
5 to 6 green tomatoes *(These have to be hard and green, not even a little red.)*
½ cup white cornmeal
3 tablespoons flour
1 to 2 cups water, soymilk, or milk
Salt and pepper, to taste
Tamari or hot coffee, to taste

Heat some oil in a cast-iron skillet. Slice the tomatoes and coat both sides with the cornmeal. Fry the slices until they are soft inside and crispy outside, but not burnt.

When you have taken the last slice from the pan, sprinkle in the flour and let it cook a few minutes until brown. Then stir in the liquid, a touch of salt and pepper, and a bit of tamari or black coffee.

(Don't forget to make the grits!)

Aunt Josephina's Fried Apples

Yield: 6 servings

The sweetener, miso, and lemon can be altered to your individual taste. I normally leave the jar of syrup and the lemon by the stove and add as I lick the spoon. Patsy says this tastes best eaten in big bites right from the skillet—or one bite at a time, snatched at weak moments straight from the fridge.

Use either:

8 to 10 thin-skinned green apples
1 to 2 teaspoons toasted sesame oil
2 tablespoons honey
3 tablespoons maple syrup or brown sugar
1 to 2 tablespoons dark miso
Soy margarine, to taste

or:

8 to 10 tart apples
4 tablespoons soy margarine
Juice of 1 lemon
⅓ to ½ cup brown sugar

Either recipe uses the same directions.

Cut the apples into either quarters or nice-sized slices. Cut away the core and leave the peels on. Heat the oil or 4 tablespoons margarine in a skillet over low heat. When it's hot, add the apples and stir around. While they are cooking, mix the maple syrup or brown sugar, miso, and lemon juice into a paste and add either that or the $1/3$ to $1/2$ cup brown sugar and lemon juice to the apples. Usually about now I throw in about $1/2$ stick of margarine just to be grandmotherly. Cover and cook over low heat for about an hour or so. Stir to keep from sticking when you have to.

Tofu "Country Ham" and Redeye Gravy

Yield: 3 to 4 servings

For this to work good you have to have firm tofu. If it seems too soft, let it sit in a colander to drain. No, this is not exactly like country ham, but it is close—hot, greasy, and salty—YUM! This is excellent leftover in a cold biscuit for a sack lunch (that's a paper bag to you Yankees).

For quick country ham flavor, spread a slice of tofu with soy margarine and a little dark miso, and put under the broiler until bubbly or caramelized.

¼ cup tamari
¼ cup water
1 tablespoon dark miso
3 tablespoons toasted sesame oil
1 tablespoon Dijon mustard
1 clove garlic, pressed
1 pound firm tofu
3 to 4 tablespoons oil
1 to 2 cups strong black coffee

Combine the tamari, water, miso, oil, mustard, and garlic in a small bowl. At this point, depending on my mood, I might stir in about 1 or 2 teaspoons of any ONE of the following ingredients: horseradish, poppy seeds, chili powder, ginger, Pick-a-Peppa Sauce (see p. 28), ketchup, Old Bay Crab Seasoning, you get the picture. Stir this together in a measuring cup, and set aside to use as a marinade.

Cut the tofu into cubes, and spread them in a shallow, non-metallic plate, like a glass pie plate. Pour the marinade over the tofu, and let sit for 2 hours or as long as you can.

Heat the oil in a skillet, and carefully add the tofu with a slotted spoon so the oil won't spatter. Add a little of the marinade, and let cook on medium heat until most of the liquid has cooked away and all sides of the cubes are brown and crispy. Don't stir—rather move them around or turn with a spatula. This does not need a lot of standing over—best to just let it cook and turn it occasionally.

When the tofu is well browned, remove it from the skillet and add the rest of the marinade. Let this come to a boil, and scrape any tofu off the bottom of the skillet. Add the coffee, return to a boil, and remove from the heat. Now you have redeye gravy. This is not a thick gravy but one that needs a biscuit to sop into it.

Okra a Go-Go

Yield: 4 to 5 servings

How can you tell if okra is tender? If you can puncture the pod easily with your thumbnail, it's edible. Thanks for this recipe goes to Marjorie K. Rawling's Cross Creek Cookery, *the best cookbook I have ever read.*

1 quart salted boiling water
1 to 2 pounds fresh, tender okra

Have the salted boiling water ready. Quickly wash the okra, leaving the stem ends on. Add the okra to the water, and let cook exactly 7 minutes after the water comes back to a boil—not a minute more or less. Drain immediately and arrange in a circle around a bowl of your favorite dip or dressing. (My favorite is blue cheese.) Hot soy margarine, lemon, and garlic works well also.

Whether you're having dip or not, this is the best way to cook okra. If you like, you can just pile the okra on a serving plate, add a few pats of soy margarine, and dig in. Hold the okra by the stem end, and eat the tender part. It's a great finger food.

Old-Time Corn Pones

Yield: 5 servings

These are a must with vegetable soup, collards, or any greens to sop up the potlikker. With some soy margarine and honey or jam, it'll cure a sweet tooth. This recipe has probably not changed a lick since a pioneer woman wrapped up a couple of pones and a few apples for her man to take to the field with him.

2¼ cups white cornmeal *(please, no yellow cornmeal for this!)*
2 to 3 tablespoons toasted sesame oil
1 cup buttermilk *(can be half milk, half water)*
1½ teaspoons baking powder
1 teaspoon salt

Put the dry ingredients into a bowl, and blend well. Make a well in the middle, and add the buttermilk and oil all at once. Stir up completely and quickly. Put big spoonfuls onto a hot, barely greased griddle over low heat. When brown on one side, turn over and let brown on the other; don't keep turning these back and forth. Keep an oven-proof platter in a slow oven to keep the pones hot as they get done. (This also helps finish cooking them.)

Woodland Avenue Tomato Sandwiches

It's best to make a big plate of these 'cause you just can't stop eating them. They are perfect for lunch or dinner in the hot, dog days of August when tomatoes are coming in.

3 to 4 tomatoes *(If you can't pick these from your backyard, let the store-bought ones sit on your windowsill for a couple of days.)*
Salt-risen bread*
Mayonnaise
Salt and pepper

The secret of this sandwich is that the bread must be sliced as thinly as possible. If you want, you can buy thinly sliced bread, or just re-slice a piece or two. This may sound hard, but it's not really. I'll tell you the easiest way. First of all, use a good serrated bread knife. Also, fresh bread won't work; the best is a few days old. And lastly, bend down so that you are eye level with what you are doing. This makes all the difference in the world.

Spread each piece of bread generously with mayo, and top with 2 or 3 slices of tomatoes, depending on how big they are.

Be sure to salt the tomatoes now. Top the other piece of bread with mayo too.

*Salt risen bread: This is an old-time Southern delicacy that even my grandmothers never attempted to make; they reminisced about their mothers making it. Some bakeries and grocery stores in the South still carry it, and there would be a serious uprising if they ever stopped. This is the one food I stock up on when I go to East Tennessee. It was so funny once, going through the airline checkpoint and having five loaves of bread stashed in my suitcase.

It's difficult to think anything but pleasant thoughts while eating a homegrown tomato.

Louis Grizzard

When I picked the first big, ripe juicy tomato of the season, I was so proud of what I'd done that I refused to let anyone cut it up until I'd paraded it around the entire neighborhood so that everyone else could see.

Duane G. Newcomb

Tomato Sandwiches

Everyone has their weakness and mine is tomato sandwiches. I go insane for them. And oh, I am so picky; if I can't have salt-risen bread sliced in two thin pieces, then it must be Pepperidge Farm X-Thin Sliced Whole Wheat. Nothing else will do. The mayo must be just so and the tomatoes sliced and peeled just right or I'll pout.

I have always heard that people will come to blows over their bar-be-que. Well, people are even more opinionated about their tomato sandwiches. And what to drink with them: plain milk, buttermilk, or Pepsi with peanuts!

The most unusual sandwich ingredient I ever saw came from Southern Living; *they recommend a sink! To be used for those tomato dribbles running down your arms.*

Here are a few additions to the Beloved Tomato Sandwich. I would probably add a few very thin slices of red onion to each of these so I won't write that on every one.

With all these choices, why are you sitting there? Why not go out in the backyard and pick you a "big old good'n" right now?

Additions to a tomato sandwich

- Roasted garlic mayo
- Good-tasting nutritional yeast flakes
- Pesto
- Potato chips
- Pickles
- Vegetarian bacon
- "Fried Chicken" Tofu, p. 29
- Mustard
- Grilled onions
- Very thinly sliced cucumbers
- Sesame salt
- Sliced avocado
- Sprouts
- Sweet banana peppers
- Fresh lettuce

Tempest Side Spoon Bread

Yield: 4 servings

Spoon bread is about as old-timey good eatin' as you can get. I'm sure many pioneers served it as highfalutin Sunday best. I best describe it as cornmeal soufflé, which does no justice to the juicy, rich finished product. Most spoon bread makers have a secret recipe; this is mine and it's unbeatable.

2 cups boiling water
1 teaspoon salt
1 cup white cornmeal *(must be white, not yellow)*
1 cup soymilk or milk
2 tablespoons oil
2 teaspoons baking powder
2 eggs *(egg replacer won't work here, but Egg Beaters will)*

Preheat the oven to 400°F. Let the water come to a boil, add the salt, and slowly stir in the cornmeal so the cornmeal won't lump. If it does, whisk it good.

Stir in the milk, then the oil and baking powder. Beat the eggs in one at a time, and stir real good. Continue whisking.

Grease a deep 8 x 8-inch casserole or soufflé dish. (Remember, this will rise some.) Bake for about 40 to 45 minutes. While this is cooking, don't keep opening the oven door and peeking in, or it will fall! The spoon bread is done when it's puffed up and golden on top. Serve immediately with collards and/or black-eyed peas. It can be served in the same dish it was cooked in.

Flawless Cornbread

Yield: 4 to 5 servings

What would we do without cornbread? I make this at least twice a week, and that's not enough. This is a dream of a recipe and can be used for corn muffins or corn sticks as well as cooked in a skillet.

Is there anything that doesn't go with cornbread? Soup, vegetables, potatoes, beans, and with jam as a dessert. Is it possible to make collards (or any greens for that matter) and not make cornbread to go along with them? Summer or winter, dinner or breakfast, this recipe is a staple.

4 to 5 tablespoons corn oil
2 cups cornmeal *(once again, white cornmeal only, please)*
1 teaspoon salt
3 teaspoons baking powder
⅓ cup whole wheat flour
1 teaspoon baking soda, if using buttermilk
1 cup soymilk, sour soymilk, or buttermilk
1 egg or egg replacer *(optional)*

Preheat the oven to 375°F. Put 1 tablespoon of the corn oil in a 10-inch cast-iron skillet, and put the skillet in the oven while it warms up. Mix the dry ingredients in a bowl, and make a well in it. Mix the wet ingredients together, and pour into the well. Stir well.

Take the hot skillet out of the oven, and tilt it so the oil runs all around the sides. Pour the batter into the skillet, and return it to the oven. (If the batter seems dry, don't worry; it's supposed to be.) Turn the heat down to 350°F, and bake for about 30 minutes. Remove the skillet and run a knife around the edge of the cornbread. Turn the skillet upside down onto a serving plate, or lift the cornbread out with a spatula to a plate. Serve hot with soy margarine.

Baking Powder Biscuits

Yield: 12 to 15 biscuits

There is something about making biscuits that gets me in touch with the sisterhood of all women. Somehow I feel a bond to pioneer ladies who made biscuits while they crossed the prairie; Okie mamas who whipped up batches of biscuits in Hooverville; Southern women who couldn't conceive of breakfast without a big platter of lighter-than-air biscuits.

Needless to say, I love biscuits. They are good for breakfast or supper and can be whipped up in no time. If you have any left over, these biscuits are the best for picnic or bag lunches. Try them split in half with soy sausage, "fried chicken" tofu, or just soy margarine and jam.

You can use any combination of white or whole wheat flour here. Just remember, the lighter the flour, the lighter the biscuit.

2 cups flour
4 teaspoons baking powder
½ teaspoon salt
4 tablespoons soy margarine
¾ cup soymilk, milk, or water

Stir the dry ingredients together, and work the margarine in with a fork until it's crumbly. Make a well in the dry ingredients, and add the liquid all at once. Stir this quickly, just until the dough leaves the sides of the bowl. This shouldn't take more than 30 seconds.

Preheat the oven to 450°F. Turn the dough onto a well-floured board, and gently knead for about 30 to 40 seconds, just until you can roll out the dough without it sticking. Roll the dough to about ½ inch thick, and cut with a biscuit cutter or cookie cutter. (Even the end of a small glass will work.)

Put these on an ungreased cookie sheet, and bake about 10 to 12 minutes, or until nice and brown on the bottom.

Three Sisters Pineapple Upside Down Cake

Yield: 6 to 8 servings

I have used just about any kind of sweetener successfully in this recipe—honey, brown sugar, maple sugar, even molasses—but this is one of the few recipes where I use brown sugar mixed with honey.

Topping:

4 tablespoons soy margarine
½ to 1 cup your favorite sweetener
4 to 5 slices fresh or canned pineapple
½ cup whole pecans

Melt the margarine and sweetener very slowly together in the bottom of a 10-inch cast-iron skillet. When this has melted, arrange the pineapple slices and pecans in the skillet, making sure this looks good, as it will be the top of the finished cake.

Batter:

¼ cup soy margarine
½ cup plus 2 tablespoons sweetener
1 egg or egg replacer
1½ cups unbleached white or whole wheat
    flour
2½ teaspoons baking powder
½ teaspoon salt
¼ cup evaporated milk mixed with ¼ cup
    water, or ½ cup of the juice from the
    canned pineapple
½ teaspoon vanilla

Preheat the oven to 350°F. Cream the margarine and the sweetener, then add the egg. Stir the dry ingredients together, and add alternately to the creamed ingredients with the milk mixture or pineapple juice. Stir in the vanilla. Pour the batter carefully over the fruit in the skillet, and bake for about 45 minutes or until it tests done in the middle.

Get a good, dependable potholder and the plate you're going to be serving the cake on. Use one of your best plates because after you see how wonderful it looks, you'll wish you had. Run a knife around the edge of the skillet to separate it from the cake. Now, place the dish directly on top of it, face down. Grip the handle of the skillet. With one hand on the plate, flip the whole thing over in one big motion. The skillet should come right off. Do this in front of someone, and they will be wildly impressed. (If any part of the cake does stick, just remove it with a spatula and fit it back where it came from.)

Stickies & Granny's Kitchen

My first real encounter with stealth must have been at one of Granny's backyard picnics, the 4th of July probably. There was always a big turnout with lots of aunts, uncles, and cousins. Shorty did the steaks on the grill, the grown-ups all played croquet, and Granny basically just ran around counting and recounting people to make sure she had enough plates, glasses, knives, napkins, and such put out.

Us kids were left to run wild, which consisted mainly of fighting over the hammock until someone finally got hurt and we weren't allowed to Play There Anymore—or playing in the old Studebaker parked in the garage. It hadn't been started in at least ten years or so, but it still had its place, lined up with the rest of the cars. (It had the most wonderful old earthen leather smell.)

My favorite game was sneaking up the back steps to sneak a stickie. When the tables were all set and it seemed like Granny might possibly have come up with a total, that meant it was safe to start up the steps.

Now you have to understand, this was a long, creaky wooden staircase in full view of the whole backyard—flower garden, croquet court, grill, and all. The added danger was the fact that two years earlier we'd eaten all the stickies before dinner and weren't even allowed to go Near That Kitchen. We were educating ourselves in the fine art of stealth and motivated by the powder of sugar (a double whammy if there ever was one). Not just sugar but Granny Sugar. When we finally made it to the kitchen, it was like we had died and gone to Candy Land. There were brownies, blackberry pie, praline cookies, cheesecake (we called it white pie), red velvet cake, and stickies. It took a few minutes just to let your eyes feast on all that food and figure out which stickie you could take without the plate looking cock-eyed. I got to be very sneaky at this. Mama was always walk-ing silently in on me, causing my heart to practically stop beating and forcing me to drop my stickie in mid-air. You could normally hear Granny coming, as she was usually talk-ing to herself, "Bettie and Bernie, that makes 19 and 20, Susan and Bill, 21, 22 . . . "

It was like those stickies had some kind of voodoo spell on me. I just couldn't stay away. I have made these many times since, but like Granny's creamed corn, it just cannot be duplicated. I think it has a lot to do with her kitchen.

Stickies

Yield: 12 stickies

Stickies are usually made up of the bits of dough left over after you've made a pie. If you haven't made a pie and want to have a little sweet pastry anyway, here's how:

2 cups flour
1 teaspoon salt
½ cup plus 3 tablespoons soy margarine
4 to 5 teaspoons ice water
½ to ¼ cup brown sugar
Cinnamon

Preheat the oven to 325°F. Mix the flour and salt, cut in the ½ cup margarine, and roll out like you would a pie crust. (If you don't know how, see p. 78) Sprinkle the brown sugar over the top. You can use honey or maple syrup, but it will be messier and even stickier, if that's possible. Dot with the 3 tablespoons margarine, and sprinkle with a dash of cinnamon. Roll up into a thick roll like a cigar. Then slice the roll into ¼ to ½-inch pieces.

Place the slices close together on a cookie sheet, so they wont come apart. Bake for about 30 minutes. Take these out of the pan while they are still warm or they will stick badly.

Half-Moon Pies/Fried Pies

Yield: 12 pies

When my grandmother Sarah reminisces about food, the first thing she usually brings up is her mother's half-moon pies. "She was bad to make some fried apple pies, slice the apples into rings, and put them out on the roof to dry. Mine just don't hold a candle to hers," she says. "Not as flaky, not as juicy, they just aren't Mamma's."

When I hear Sarah say this, it just can't be true, for her fried apple pies are one of the Seven Wonders of the World—perfection in each and every mouthful.

These pies can be made with apples or peaches, and it generally depends on what part of the country you come from as to how you remember them. The deeper into the South you go, the more people eat peach fried pies.

Pastry:
2 cups flour
1 teaspoon salt
½ teaspoon baking powder
¾ cup hot soymilk
½ cup shortening *(soy margarine for you healthy people)*

Filling:
2 cups dried apple or peach slices
2 cups water
½ cup brown sugar
Peanut oil for frying *(Use peanut oil for its
  delicious flavor and the fact that it does
  better at the high temperatures you use
  while frying.)*

Sift the flour, salt, and baking powder together. In another bowl, mix the hot milk and margarine until the margarine is almost melted. Add the flour mixture a little at a time, and mix gently with a fork. When just blended, pat into a ball, wrap in plastic, and refrigerate for 2 hours or overnight.

For the filling, cook the apples or peaches in the water at a boil for a few minutes, then turn down and let simmer for about an hour. If you need to add a little more water, it's fine, but don't add too much. The apples should have a thick, jam-like consistency. Either let this come to room temperature or put it in the fridge. Don't try to make pies and fry them while the fruit is hot.

When you are ready to make the pies, take the pastry out of the fridge and let sit about 30 minutes or so. Divide into about 12 balls, flatten, and roll out about 6 inches across with a rolling pin.

Heap about 2 tablespoons of fruit onto 1 half of each circle. Fold the top over the fruit, meeting the other half and making a half moon. Turn up the edge a little bit if you need to, and crimp with a fork. Moisten the edges a little with cold water, if you need it while crimping, to make sure they are sealed well. You don't want the juice to run out and splatter in the hot oil.

Heat some oil in a cast-iron skillet. When hot, gently put in the pies a few at a time. Don't crowd the pies in the skillet. When golden perfection is achieved on one side, gently turn over on the other side, and let fry until also golden.

Remove to paper towels or a cooling rack. Let cool just enough to keep from burning your tongue before eating.

Great-Grandmother's Shortcake

Yield: 5 to 6 servings

These are glorious little things, not at all like you remember from the grocery store. I like to serve a big bowl of berries and a big bowl of these little shortcakes, so that my guests can stack them four high if they like (and they do).

2 cups unbleached all-purpose or pastry
    flour
1 teaspoon baking powder
Pinch of salt
2 tablespoons honey or sugar
½ cup soy margarine
½ cup soymilk or milk

Sift the dry ingredients together, then work the margarine in with a fork until crumbly. Add the milk and quickly stir with a fork until the dough leaves the side of the bowl. Roll the dough as thinly as possible, and cut out with a large cookie cutter. If you don't have one, you can use a wide-mouth jar.

Preheat the oven to 450°F. Barely oil the top of a cut-out round, and put another one on top of it. Place on a greased cookie sheet. Do all of these little rounds the same way, 2 high. Bake for 8 to 12 minutes until brown. Remove from the oven and separate the tops from the bottoms immediately.

Vegetables

Life is too short to stuff a mushroom.
                Shirley Conran, *Superwoman*

You should give yourself plenty of time; you should work on it with nothing in your mind, and without expecting anything. You should just cook!
                Shunryu Suzuki,.
                Zen Mind, Beginners Mind

Beans hit cornbread on the head
Cornbread say, "I'm almost dead."
Beans tell cornbread: "Get up man,
We go together hand and hand."
                Louis Jordan

Bowls

I have this thing about bowls. I love them. It's very safe to say I am a bowl maniac, a bowl-a-holic. I think it may have been my love of bowls that made me get into cooking in the first place. I cannot pass a bowl at a flea market; it calls to me. Even though I have more bowls than I will ever need in a lifetime, my bowl craving is never satisfied.

The pantry where I keep my bowls is my favorite room of the house. It was the first room I painted, although all the other rooms needed painting more. My husband said, "Why are you spending so much time on that room? No one will ever see it." "It's for the bowls," I said, as if I were talking about a secret lover. I keep a little stool in the pantry so I can go in and sit with the bowls. I always emerge feeling much more relaxed and much happier. They have such happy colors and patterns, like balloons of hope floating on the shelves.

There are white Fire Kings with black or red polkadots, the big turquoise Fiesta one with a lid my sister gave me, the set of what I call Martha Stewart green, and the clear glass ones that are so good for salads. There's the set of smaller graduated bowls with lids that I have stacked so they look like a castle. Oh, the set of alternating maroon and pink (I always put the cranberry frappe in the maroon and the beets in the pink), and a truly wonderful one that is light blue with the north wind blowing around it, so good for soup on a hot day. There are milk glass mixing bowls and the set with the fruit painted on. And oh, the divided ones, how could I ever forget the divided ones?

And the weird part is that even with this love of bowls, I still have a bowl prejudice. I am so partial to a particular set that I have to use it and only it for certain things. You know the one I mean. The set of four—the biggest one is yellow, then green, then red, and the smallest one is blue. How could a kitchen be a kitchen without these particular bowls? The potato salad always tastes better in the big yellow one. Cole slaw goes in the green one. The red one is usually missing from most people's sets. My mother says it's the one most people use to feed the dog; it sits on the floor and is most likely to be tripped over and broken. The blue one is almost like some sort of a homeopathic cure. If you are making soup for a sick person, even yourself, can you imagine reaching for any bowl other than that small blue one? Once at a flea market, I found a variation of this set. The big one was red, then blue, green, and yellow. I felt like I had found the four-leaf clover of the bowl world. My lucky bowls.

If you don't have a "special bowl," the next time you visit your mama's, granny's, or favorite maiden aunt, ask them to part with one they may have stuck in the back of the pantry. Keep it in a place where you'll see it often, and reach for it regularly. Let it be your connection to the generations of women before you who have reached for a bowl just like you are now. Let it inspire you and remind you that life itself was probably started in a big mixing bowl. When you fill a bowl, it is not just filling your stomach, it's filling your heart. It is filling your soul.

Sweetwater Scalloped Tomatoes

Yield: 3 to 4 servings

In about the second week of August, my house is taken hostage by tomatoes. They cover all the counters, the washer, the dryer, the kitchen table, the window sills, the hood of whichever car is in the carport—they are everywhere you look. I'm always looking for a new way to use them. Here is a great one.

5 to 6 slices vegetarian bacon
Oil or soy margarine, as needed
1 small onion, chopped
⅓ cup bread crumbs
3 to 4 medium tomatoes

Cook the vegetarian bacon in a little of the oil, and set aside. Cook the onion in same oil as the bacon. When the onions are done, add the bread crumbs and let cook a few more minutes.

Arrange the sliced tomatoes on a pie plate. Cover with the onion and bread crumb mixture and then the crumbled pieces of vegetarian bacon. Put under the broiler for just a few minutes until the tomatoes are heated through.

Corn "Oysters"

Yield: 6 side dish servings

These are a good side dish with just about anything. I like to top off a salad with 2 or 3 of these "oysters." They are delicious!

⅔ cup flour
¾ teaspoon baking powder
½ teaspoon salt
⅓ cup soymilk
Egg replacer equal to 1 egg
2 cups corn kernels
Safflower or olive oil, as needed

Combine the flour, baking powder, salt, soymilk, and egg replacer in a blender or food processor. Blend until just smooth. Pour in a bowl and add the corn. Generously cover the bottom of a skillet with oil, and heat on the stovetop. When hot, add a tablespoon of batter one at a time. Cook until golden brown on the bottom, about 2 to 3 minutes. Brown the other side. Remove from the skillet and keep warm until all the "oysters" are done.

Hash Browns

Yield: 4 to 5 servings

Why do hash browns always taste best at some greasy spoon 100 miles from nowhere? Some meals are not complete without a side of potatoes. Come to think of it, I make whole meals of just fried potatoes. If I am ever making potatoes for anything, I make a lot because I know I can use any leftovers for hash browns. This is the way I do it. You'll need:

4 to 6 medium or large potatoes *(leftover boiled or baked potatoes work well)*
Olive oil
½ to 1 onion, finely chopped
1 clove garlic, smashed and chopped
Plenty of salt and pepper

Boil the potatoes whole and let cool, at least enough to handle. Chop into cubes, then cover the bottom of a cast-iron skillet with oil. Heat the oil and add the chopped onion. Let cook a few minutes, then add the potatoes. This is the secret: Don't pile too many potatoes in the skillet, just make 2 pans at once; they will taste better.

Salt and pepper generously and cook over medium heat. Turn with a spatula after cooking 5 minutes or so. The bottoms should be brown and crispy. Let the other side cook until they are done the way you like them. Drizzle on a little more oil if you need to.

For a fancier dish, add a few chopped mushrooms and half a chopped green pepper when adding the onion. I almost forgot, a little sage or paprika sprinkled over the top when cooking is really yummy.

Nora's Corn Pudding

Yield: 6 to 8 servings

Corn pudding is so soothing, so satisfying, it is in a category way beyond comfort food. I mean, it was comfort food to the Pilgrims. It's like sunshine in a casserole dish. My kitchen is too hot to make this in the summer, so I cut lots of corn off the cob, freeze it, and make this all winter. It is just as good. Be sure to get the best sweet corn you can find; it makes a big difference. If cutting the corn off the cob, be sure to score and milk the cob too. (See Granny's Creamed Corn, p. 54.) No, this recipe doesn't have eggs, butter, or milk but is delicious none the same.

2 tablespoons soy margarine

1 teaspoon toasted sesame oil

1 onion, finely chopped

½ small, very mild chili, seeded and finely chopped

⅓ pound soft tofu

1 cup water

1½ teaspoons vegetarian broth powder

1 cup soymilk

Egg replacer equivalent to 3 eggs

1 teaspoon salt

Several good shakes of pepper

¼ cup sugar

1 dozen ears fresh corn (4 cups kernels after they're cut off the cob), or two 16-ounce bags frozen sweet corn

3 tablespoons finely chopped chives

In a skillet, melt the margarine and sesame oil. When nice and hot, add the onion and chili. While cooking, process everything else except the corn and chives in a blender or food processor until smooth. When the onions are tender, add the blender mixture. Let cook a few minutes, then add the corn.

Preheat the oven to 350°F. Let the mixture cook slowly for about 10 to 15 minutes. Stir in the chives last. Pour into a 9 x 13-inch baking dish, and bake for 45 minutes. Fancy people bake this in a water bath, but I never do and it comes out fine.

Old Fashioned Potato Pancakes

Yield: 4 to 5 servings

I always make way too many mashed potatoes just so I can make this the next day. These potato cakes are different from Northern-style ones that are grated, fried, and served with applesauce or sour cream. If you like roasted garlic, spread it on the top of this like butter when you serve it.

3 cups leftover mashed potatoes
1 small onion, grated
1 clove garlic, crushed
Egg replacer equal to 2 eggs *(If dry egg replacer is used, reconstitute with soymilk.)*
¼ teaspoon each salt and pepper
Oil or soy margarine, as needed

Mix all the ingredients in a big bowl. Heat the oil or margarine in a skillet over medium heat. Drop the potato mixture (it should be very soft) gently into the hot oil or margarine. Let brown on one side, then flip and brown on the other. Serve with salad or just about any vegetable. At breakfast, serve with vegetarian bacon and soy sausage.

Jack Cornett's Copper Pennies

Yield: 8 servings

This is a wonderful way to make carrots and has a real lip-smacking quality. It is one of my grandmother's specialties.

2 pounds carrots
1 teaspoon Grey Poupon or Dijon mustard
⅔ cup sugar, or ⅓ cup maple syrup and ⅓ cup sugar
One 10-ounce can tomato soup concentrate
½ cup olive oil
¼ cup balsamic vinegar
1 small green pepper, very thinly sliced
1 medium red onion, sliced very thinly in half moons

Slice the carrots into small circles Steam about 10 minutes, until just barely done, but not crunchy. Don't let the carrots get too soft.

While the carrots are cooking, mix the mustard and sugar together first, then add the liquids. Add the hot carrots and uncooked pepper and onion, and stir to combine. This is best after sitting a few days.

Church Suppler Caramelized Onions

Yield: 4 servings

Onion lovers, gather round, as you are in for a real treat. This is the kind of recipe where I find myself in the kitchen, licking the juices left in the bottom of the baking dish when all the guests have gone home. The sugars in the onions mix with the sweetness of the balsamic vinegar. I get chills up my spine in anticipation of each bite. Maybe this wouldn't be so good for church after all!

1 cup balsamic vinegar
2 large red or Vidalia onions, skinned and
    cut in half or crosswise
2 tablespoons soy margarine
¾ cup chopped pecans
¼ cup packed brown sugar

Preheat the oven to 400°F. In a saucepan, bring the vinegar to a boil, then remove from the heat. Pour into a 8 x 8-inch baking dish. Place the onions cut side down in the dish, and bake for 55 minutes or until the onions are the color of dark chocolate.

Melt the margarine in a skillet over medium heat, and add the pecans, stirring often. After about 2 minutes, add the brown sugar. Continue stirring and cooking until bubbly. Serve the onions cut side up, drizzling the sauce and nuts over the top.

If you want to fix all this in an electric skillet, it works great. Let the vinegar come to a boil in the skillet. Add the onions, cover, and let cook for 1 hour at 300°F to 325°F. Check it occasionally to see if the liquid has cooked off before the onions are done. Add more liquid if needed.

Onion Shortcake

Yield: 4 to 5 servings

This is a good dish to have instead of mashed potatoes and gravy or biscuits and gravy.

4 to 5 onions, chopped
½ cup oil

Biscuit dough:
2 cups whole wheat flour
4 teaspoons baking powder
½ teaspoon salt
4 tablespoons oil or soy margarine
½ to ⅔ cup soymilk

3 tablespoons soy margarine
3 tablespoons chick-pea, rice, or whole
    wheat flour
1 tablespoon miso dissolved in 1 cup
    soymilk or water

Sauté the onions in the ½ cup oil; when they are soft, set them aside until you are ready for them.

Mix the dry ingredients for the biscuit dough, cutting in the oil or margarine with 2 knives. Add the soymilk and stir just enough to combine the ingredients, then turn the dough out and knead a few times. Press this into a greased 8 x 8-inch casserole dish, and spread the cooled onions over the dough.

Preheat the oven to 400°F. To make the sauce, melt the 3 tablespoons margarine in the same pan used to cook the onions. Add the 3 tablespoons flour, and make a paste. Add the dissolved miso to the paste, and stir it in; remove from the heat. You can add a touch of tamari if you have it. Pour this over the onions, and bake for about 15 to 20 minutes or until the dough is done.

Matilda's Summer Squash

Yield: 4 to 5 servings

This is my favorite vegetable recipe. The colors are wonderful and the onions get so sweet you won't believe it. You can pile this up a little bit when you're layering it, as the tomatoes and squash will shrink considerably.

If you can't get homegrown, red-ripe tomatoes and have to settle for supermarket tomatoes, let them sit in the window for a couple of days to ripen up a bit.

4 yellow summer squash (about 1½ pounds)
2 red or yellow onions
3 to 4 big, red, ripe-from-the-backyard
    tomatoes
A few dots of soy margarine
1 teaspoon dried basil
Salt, to taste
Parmesan or soy Parmesan, to taste
½ to 1 cup bread crumbs

Slice the vegetables into thin rounds, and layer in a 9 x 13-inch casserole dish, sprinkling the tomato layer with the basil and salt. Dot the squash layer with the margarine. If you ever eat Parmesan cheese, now is the time. Just sprinkle some on when you do the margarine.

Preheat the oven to 350°F. Continue layering until the ingredients are used up. Make the last layer one of bread crumbs and dots of soy margarine. Bake for about an hour or until the squash is tender.

Granny's Famous Creamed Corn

Yield: 6 servings

I think one of Granny's secrets is that she always uses sweet white corn like Silver Queen. She gets lots in the summer, cuts it off the cob, and freezes it. We enjoy creamed corn all winter long. When I go to Granny's for dinner, she makes a huge bowl of creamed corn and puts it right on my plate. Isn't it nice to be indulged?

6 to 8 ears corn, scored and milked
    (5 to 6 cups)
3 tablespoons soy margarine
¼ to ⅓ cup flour
2 tablespoons honey
½ cup soymilk or milk *(water will do)*
½ teaspoon salt
Black pepper, to taste

To score corn, run a knife through the kernels before cutting off the cob. To milk it, hold the corn over a bowl and run the edge of a spoon over what is left after the kernels are cut off the cob.

Cut the corn off the cob into a bowl. (You don't want to waste any of the juice.) Melt the margarine in a pan, and stir in the flour, then the honey. Let this cook a few minutes, then add the corn with its juice. Give it a stir and add the liquid, salt, and pepper. Stir this occasionally; it shouldn't take long to thicken. Put a few dots of soy margarine on top, and serve immediately.

Mexican Beans

Yield: 6 to 8 servings

These beans are great in burritos, enchiladas, quesadillas, or as a side dish to any Mexican meal. Don't stop there though; sopping up the juice of the beans with a piece of cornbread or hushpuppy is what it's all about.

It's nice to throw in a handful of red beans in this also. Remember, beans triple in size so don't cook too many. Savory is especially good in Mexican beans and is supposed to help make the beans less "musical."

2 to 3 cups dry beans *(pintos or red beans are good)*
4 to 6 cups water, or as needed
¼ cup oil
2 to 3 teaspoons savory
2 to 3 teaspoons cumin
1 teaspoon cayenne
2 to 3 teaspoons oregano
2 cloves garlic
Several dashes Tabasco
2 onions, chopped
Salt, to taste

Soak the beans overnight in enough water to cover. Rinse them well, put them in a deep pot, and cover generously with water. Add everything except the onions and salt. Let come to a boil for a few minutes, then cover, turn down the heat, and simmer about 2 hours. Stir every so often, and add more water when you need to. When the beans feel soft, add the onions and salt and let them finish cooking uncovered.

If you have half a jar of tomato juice sitting around, pour that in. Or if you have a few ripe tomatoes sitting in the window, chop them up and throw them in. Run some water in the bottom of a ketchup bottle, swish it around, and pour that in too. If you don't have any of these things, no problem; your beans will still be good.

Let the beans cook another hour or so until they get really juicy. Don't forget to add more water if you have to. Cover and let sit until dinnertime. I like the beans just like this, though some people I know like to put them in the blender and make a nice taco filling.

Fresh Corn or Vegetable Fritters

Yield: 4 to 6 servings

You do not have to just use corn in these fritters. You can use almost any vegetable. Grated zucchini, chopped scallions, and mushrooms all work well. Once I used fresh peas and they were delicious.

I have never been much of a pancake eater, but I can eat corn fritters by the half-dozen. This is another one of those recipes that sounds too easy to be good; trust me, . . . don't worry if the first few stick and tear up. You usually have to sacrifice a few to the great fritter god in the sky. Also, these fritters are good to make for breakfast, served crispy hot with maple syrup poured over and vegetarian bacon on the side.

1 cup flour
1 cup water, milk, beer, or mineral water
1 teaspoon baking powder
Touch of honey
¼ cup oil
2 eggs or egg replacer
½ onion, finely chopped *(optional)*
Salt and pepper, to taste
1½ to 2 cups corn, chopped kale, spinach, grated carrots, zucchini, leftover noodles, mashed potatoes, onions, etc.
Oil for frying

Completely mix all the ingredients in a bowl so there are no lumps. Stir in the vegetables last. Get your skillet good and hot, but don't turn it up as high as it will go, because this causes the outside of the fritters to brown while the inside stays doughy. This is a thin batter; I like mine that way.

Put a little oil in the skillet. You don't want to fry these; you want just enough oil so the fritter won't stick. Pour in some batter with a tablespoon. I usually push in the edges of the fritter back with a spatula so I can get 2 or 3 in the skillet at the same time. If you are making a lot, use 2 skillets, as it will go twice as fast. These cook just like pancakes; when the tops are covered with little air holes, turn them over and let them brown on the other side. The last ones always come out best.

Butter Beans

Yield: 4 to 6 servings

Even the ultra-mod B-52's will proudly exclaim, "Everybody likes butter beans!" This simple fare is what comfort is all about. Forget mashed potatoes, butter beans reign supreme as the ultimate comfort food. Be sure to make them with plenty of water, as the potlikker (juice) is the best part. You can sop it up with cornbread or serve it over rice. I usually eat all the beans from my bowl and then drink the juice all down at once. The Southern equivalent of power drinks!

You may find speckled butter beans, baby limas, or something called sivvy beans. They all cook the same, delicious!

1 quart of water
3 cups freshly shelled butter beans
Salt, to taste
A couple of pats of soy margarine

Put the water and beans in a large pot, let come to a boil, and simmer for 30 minutes to 2 hours, partially covered, depending on your taste, the size of the beans, etc. The beans should be buttery and soft when pressed with the back of a spoon. Toward the end of cooking time, add the salt and soy margarine.

Butter Beans and Corn

The only way to improve butter beans is to add fresh corn. Depending on how much beans you are making, cut the corn off 2 to 5 ears of corn and add to the beans when they are about half done. Be sure to "score and milk" the corn when you put it in. (See Granny's Creamed Corn, p. 54.)

I usually make the effort to have lots of frozen corn and butter beans on hand so in the winter I can make soup. Just start with a few onions in the pot, then add beans, potatoes or rice, and then corn. It's a whatever-you-want-to-put-in soup, as long as it has the beans and corn.

The Vegetable Man

One of the things I was lucky enough to experience in my life was Mr. Wiseman, the vegetable man. Through the years, he would appear in the driveway in an old pick-up truck, as regular as the milkman, dressed in overalls and a worn-out sport coat. With a tentative smile and a tip of his sweat-stained fedora, he would leave his bounty on the back steps. And bounty it was— sweet corn, tomatoes, string beans, butter beans, peppers, okra, potatoes, blackberries, red raspberries, rhubarb, and fresh eggs.

I still remember when I became a teenager, I raced to the phone, hoping it might be the football star of my dreams. "Hello," I would pant breathlessly into the phone.

"Is Mother there? It's Wiseman," I would hear a shaky voice ask. "Do ye need eggs?"

I must honestly admit I never gave much of a thought to Mr. Wiseman then. I just assumed all those great vegetables appeared magically out of the back of his truck. I never appreciated the hours of back-breaking work that go into a farm, much less a garden the size required for all those vegetables.

I would love to sit with Mr. Wiseman now and ask, "How do you keep the bugs off the eggplant? How do you keep the deer out of the garden? How do you keep the raccoon out of the corn? How do you keep the voles out of the carrots? Do you keep your fedora at that rakish angle even when you are plowing?"

Mr. Wiseman, I realize now, was a Super Hero Vegetable Man. He didn't just bring the vegetables. He delivered the goods.

Things to Do with Okra

Are you one of those people who thinks okra is nothing more than a slimy green vegetable that lays on the plate? Okra has history. People were eating okra in Africa before anyone had even dug a garden in America.

When choosing okra at the grocery store, go for the small pods. They are the most tender. If you aren't sure, try to pierce the pod with your thumbnail. If you can't, it's not fit to eat.

Fried Okra and Potatoes

Yield: 4 servings

This tastes good with crispy garlic cornbread.

¼ cup flour
1 tablespoon cornmeal
1 teaspoon salt
Dash of pepper
2 to 3 cups sliced okra
¾ cup cubed potatoes
Oil, as needed

Combine the flour, cornmeal, salt, and pepper in a bowl. Add the okra and potatoes, and toss well.

Cover the bottom of a skillet with oil, and heat. Add the okra and potato mixture, and turn often but gently. When the potatoes are done, it's ready. It should be brown and crispy all over.

Grilled Okra and Tomatoes

Yield: 4 to 5 servings

If you don't have a grill basket, go get one immediately. You will never have to deal with peppers or onions falling through onto the coals and going up in flames right before your eyes.

2 pounds okra
2 to 3 tablespoons oil
5 tomatoes
Salt and pepper, to taste

Put the okra in a plastic bag, and pour in the oil. Mix inside the bag until the okra is evenly covered. Put in a grill basket over a medium-hot grill. Sit the tomatoes on the edges of the grill, and turn as needed. The okra should cook for 5 to 7 minutes. When the okra is done, remove from the grill and peel the tomatoes quickly. (The peels should just about slip off.) Cut in chunks and toss with the okra. Arrange on a platter and toss with salt and pepper.

Okra Étouffée

Yield: 5 to 6 servings

1 rib celery, chopped
1 onion, chopped
1 medium green pepper, chopped
1 hot pepper, finely chopped *(optional)*
2 to 3 tablespoons olive oil
3 cups fresh okra, sliced *(Do not allow to sit a long time before cooking)*
3 fresh tomatoes, chopped
½ cup water
Pinch each of salt and pepper
Potato chips and bread crumbs *(enough of each to cover the casserole)*
Several pats soy margarine

Sauté the celery, onion, and peppers in the olive oil until soft. Add the okra and tomatoes (along with any tomato juice left from chopping), water, salt, and pepper. Let cook about 10 minutes.

Preheat the oven to 350°F. Transfer to a greased 8 x 8-inch casserole dish, loosely cover with aluminum foil, and bake for 50 minutes. Crush the potato chips and mix with the bread crumbs. Remove the casserole and dot with margarine, spread the crumb mixture over the top, and bake 15 more minutes, or until browned on top. This is real good over rice or with corn on the cob. Butter beans as a side dish would work too.

How to Bake a Squash

Cut the squash in half, remove the seeds, and lay flat side down in a baking dish in about ¼ inch of water. Bake 30 minutes at 350°F, then turn over and drop a pat of margarine into the center. Bake 30 more minutes at the same temperature. This works perfectly and keeps the squash from drying out.

Grains

Blow up your T.V.
Throw away your paper,
Move to the country
Build you a home.
Plant a little garden
Eat a lot of peaches,
Try to find Jesus
On your own.

John Prine

To me the meanest flower that blows can give
Thoughts that do often lie too deep for tears.

William Wordsworth

Johnny Reb Dirty Rice

Yield: 8 to 10 servings

This is real traditional, down-home Southern cookin' at its best. Dirty rice is usually made with chicken livers; here's how I do it. It's an easy recipe, a great change from plain rice, and is a great dish to have with tofu or tempeh, baked squash, or sweet potatoes.

1 red onion, chopped
1 bunch green onions, chopped
2 cloves garlic, smashed and chopped
1 green pepper, chopped
2 tablespoons oil
1 cup broken pecans, peanuts, or walnuts
½ teaspoon cayenne pepper

Sauce:

¼ cup tamari
2 teaspoons dry mustard
2 tablespoons sesame oil
1 tablespoon prepared horseradish

½ cup chopped parsley
4 to 5 cups cooked rice *(leftover will do fine)*
Several pats of soy margarine

Sauté the onions, garlic, and green pepper in the oil until soft. Add the nuts and cayenne pepper, and continue cooking. Combine the tamari and enough water in a measuring cup to make about ½ cup. Add the other sauce ingredients, stir well, and add to the skillet mixture. Turn down the heat and cover.

Preheat the oven to 350°F. Grease a rectangular 9 x 13-inch casserole dish. Add the parsley to the skillet mixture, and then recover. Spread the rice in the bottom of the casserole, and spread the skillet mixture over it. Dot generously with margarine, and bake for 20 minutes, or about 30 minutes if cold rice is used.

Cajun Red Beans and Rice

Yield: 12 servings

1 pound red beans or red kidney beans
2 or 3 Bermuda onions, chopped
2 cloves garlic, smashed and chopped
1 bunch scallions, chopped *(including tops)*
2 tablespoons oil
1 bunch parsley, chopped
Several stalks of celery (including leaves), chopped
½ teaspoon cayenne
6 to 8 cups steamed hot rice
Salt, to taste

Let the beans soak overnight in enough water to cover.

Sauté the onions, garlic, and half of the scallions in the oil. Rinse the beans and add to the onions, stir well, and add about 6 cups of water and the celery. Let come to a boil, then turn down and simmer about 2 hours. Check it every once and a while, and add water if necessary. Towards the end of the cooking time, stir and mash the softest beans against the edge of the pot to thicken it all up. Add the salt.

Serve the beans with a big bowl of rice and a bowl of the remaining chopped green scallions.

If you would like, you can make tofu fatback (see p. 28) and add it to these beans the last 30 minutes or so of cooking time.

Savannah Red Rice

Yield: 6 to 8 servings

Two 16-ounce cans whole tomatoes, undrained
6 slices vegetarian bacon
1 tablespoon oil
2 teaspoons toasted sesame oil
½ onion, chopped
½ cup chopped celery
½ green pepper, chopped
2 cups uncooked long grain rice
2 teaspoons salt
Dash pepper
2 shakes hot sauce

Put the tomatoes in a blender, and whirl until smooth; set aside.

Cook the vegetarian bacon in the 1 tablespoon oil, keeping the drippings in the pan. Crumble the bacon and set aside.

Cook the rest of the vegetables in the same pan as the bacon, using the toasted sesame oil and adding a little more oil if needed. When the vegetables are tender, add the tomatoes and rice, stir, and let cook 10 minutes.

Preheat the oven to 350°F. Grease a 9 x 13-inch casserole dish, and carefully spoon in the mixture. Cover and bake 1 hour. Top with the crumbled bacon before serving.

Basic Cornbread Dressing

Yield: 6 to 8 generous servings

Don't wait until Thanksgiving or Christmas to have stuffing. The ingredients are usually just sitting around in your refrigerator. This dressing really is supreme. This is a good dish to leave covered and let sit while you finish the rest of dinner.

I call this "basic" dressing because no two dressings ever come out the same. You may want to add a little leftover rice, omit the carrots, and add more nuts. Do what you like; this is a good recipe to experiment with. It's deceptively simple and also the best way ever to use your leftover cornbread. Take note—when they made stuffing at my great-grandmother Hunter's house, she could be heard to call out more than once, "Don't stir the dressing—it'll clump!"

3 tablespoons olive or sesame oil

2 cloves garlic, mashed and chopped

1 to 2 onions, diced

2 to 3 carrots, cut into match sticks

1 tablespoon sage

½ teaspoon thyme *(can add up to 1 tablespoon)*

¼ teaspoon rosemary *(can add up to 1 tablespoon)*

2 to 3 celery stalks, sliced and chopped

¼ cup water mixed with ¼ cup tamari

4 to 6 cups finely crumbled cornbread *(This can't be "Yankee" cornbread made with honey or sugar—that tastes like cake.)*

½ bunch parsley, chopped

3 tablespoons soy margarine

½ to 1 cup chopped toasted pecans, walnuts, chestnuts, sunflower seeds, or any of your favorite toasted nuts

Salt and lots of black pepper

Heat the oil in a skillet, and add the garlic, onions, carrots, herbs, and celery, in that order. Let cook over medium heat for about 10 minutes. The vegetables should be rendering a little juice. If not, or if the mixture has started to stick at any time, add the tamari-water mixture. Cover and let cook about 5 more minutes. By this time, it should be very juicy on the bottom.

Crumble the cornbread finely right into the pan. Be a little picky when doing this; large hunks aren't good. Since this is leftover, it'll be dry and will crumble easily. If you have any leftover rice, you can add this now. Barely toss this, add parsley, big pats of margarine, and chopped, roasted nuts. Turn the heat to low, cover, and let steam about 15 minutes.

For a nice change, omit any vegetable and add soy sausage. Or omit the cornbread and add wild rice, or substitute mushrooms for the carrots.

Remember though, don't stir this, rather toss gently with a spatula.

Just Plain Grits

Follow the directions according to the package. These are pretty hard to mess up. They need lots of soy margarine, and you can go from there. Don't forget the salt; it is imperative. Good-tasting nutritional yeast is great. Parmesan is also, as is chopped umeboshi plum (as a salt pork substitute, p. 11), hot sauce, toasted nuts of any kind, and even gravy. Grits are served on a plate, not a bowl. When leftover, you'll find they congeal into a cold lump. Put this in the fridge, and when ready to use again, slice it up and fry it. Yum. If you can't find grits at your grocery store, the next time you are traveling in the South, you can get a five-pound bag which ought to do you for about a year.

Fried Grits

Well, I'll tell you the secret and let you take it from there. You can make plain fried grits or get as inventive or fancy as you want. Go ahead and make grits. When done, pour into a loaf pan or a cookie sheet, and let chill overnight.

Remove from the refrigerator, and slice into fingers or squares. Dredge in flour or good-tasting nutritional yeast, if you want. Heat peanut oil in a skillet, and add the sliced grits gently so the oil won't splatter. Drizzle with tamari.

To change around or fancy it up, you could add soy cheese, nutritional yeast cheese, pesto, sesame salt, or Asian hoisan sauce when the grits are just done cooking before putting them in the fridge.

Another way to be fancy is to cut out the grits with special shaped cookie cutters.

Garlic Grits

Yield: 6 to 8 servings

What are grits anyway? Usually the grits you get from the grocery store are hominy grits—degerminated corn that has been finely ground on steel rollers. Stone ground grits are simply whole grain corn, ground very coarsely on stones. Whenever you travel in the South, be sure to buy a big bag of stone ground grits. You couldn't find a better souvenir anywhere.

1 cup grits
4½ cups water
½ teaspoon salt
½ cup soy margarine
1 egg or egg replacer
¾ cup milk or soymilk
2 cloves garlic, smashed and chopped
¾ to 1 cup grated sharp cheddar cheese or
     cheese substitute

Cook the grits in the water and salt over low heat until mushy. Stir in the margarine, egg, and milk. Next, stir in the garlic, cheese, and whatever else you want to add. Obviously, you have to stir this up quite a lot. Preheat the oven to 350°F. Pour into a 9 x 13-inch greased baking dish, and bake for 35 minutes.

Sauces and Gravies

I come from a home where gravy is a beverage.
Erma Bombeck

An onion can make people cry, but there's no vegetable that can make them laugh.
Anonymous

All About Gravy

A good pan of gravy can inspire poetry. A delicately made sauce turns a good vegetable into a sensation. This is really the time when you can use your imagination. Try a different herb or use a combination of herbs that you like. My favorite gravy happened by accident when I used chickpea flour instead of whole wheat.

On a frosty winter night, what grain is complete without a little gravy on top? Imagine a thick mustard sauce over cauliflower! I consider a biscuit almost naked if there's not something for it to sop up. Sauces are the way to win the hearts of those meat-and-potato vegetarians you know. The next time you have your parents over for dinner, make "fried chicken" tofu with mashed potatoes and gravy; your mother will wonder what she did right for a change.

Mushroom Gravy

Yield: 5 to 6 cups

1 small onion, finely chopped
2 cups chopped mushrooms
2 to 3 tablespoons soy margarine or oil
1 big handful flour *(OK, about ⅓ cup)*
2 to 3 cups soymilk or milk, depending on
    how thick you want your gravy
Tamari, salt, and pepper, to taste

Sauté the onion and mushrooms in the margarine or oil until soft. Add the flour and stir over low heat until a paste forms and the flour has had time to brown a little.

Add the soymilk and continue stirring with a whip or a fork until the mixture thickens. Add more or less liquid depending on the consistency you want. A touch of tamari, salt, and lots of black pepper and it's ready to pour over rice, potatoes, biscuits, and even toast!

Onion Marmalade

Yield: about 6 cups

This is so good, especially in the wintertime. When it's cold out, I like to cook things that warm up the house and make me feel cozy. Some people call this onion butter, and really, it is good to use just like butter. Spread on toast or corn, it's the best. A big dollop on top of a bowl of soup ain't too shabby either.

3 to 4 tablespoons olive oil
6 to 7 cups mixed red, yellow, and white
    onions, sliced in half moons
2 cloves garlic, minced
½ cup white wine or balsamic vinegar
3 teaspoons sugar
Salt and pepper, to taste

Heat the oil in large pot. Add the onions and cook very slowly, stirring often. If the onions seem too dry, add a touch more oil. After about 45 minutes to 1 hour, add the vinegar and sugar. Continue cooking on low heat until it's all soft, brown, sweet, and cozy. Season with salt and pepper.

White Sauce

Yield: 1½ to 2 cups

Here is the basic recipe for a plain white sauce from which you can build almost any sauce or gravy. The best gravy always starts with the "drippings" left in a frying pan after frying or sautéing something. Instead of rinsing out the pan, use it for the base of your sauce. If you have no drippings, use sesame or olive oil to sauté the sauce ingredients (onions, mushrooms, soy sausage, seeds, or nuts). For a more delicate herb sauce, use only soy margarine, as oil is a bit heavy, tending to hide the flavors.

As for flour, you have many choices here. Whole wheat or unbleached white flour are the old standbys. Try chick-pea flour, rice flour, or corn-meal for a change. Don't forget arrowroot, kudzu, or cornstarch as thickeners.

This is a good time to clean out your refrigerator. You may use water, soymilk, or water that was used to steam vegetables. Tomato juice is deli-cious. Don't be afraid to stir in some chutney, chili sauce, sweet and sour sauce, prepared mus-tard, vegetarian Worcestershire sauce, or hot sauce. Flat beer, wine, or sherry work too.

3 tablespoons soy margarine, sesame oil,
   or olive oil
3 tablespoons flour
1 to 1½ cups liquid

Melt the margarine over low heat in a cast-iron skillet or saucepan. Make sure it doesn't burn. Add the flour and stir until you have a nice paste. (You have just done something very French, called making a "roux.") Keep on stirring until the flour has had a little time to roast, giving it some flavor. Slowly stir in the liquid until all the lumps are gone and the mixture starts to thicken. This takes a few minutes of careful attention.

Hints

1. If your sauce just won't thicken, don't despair. In a small bowl, mix 1 table-spoon of cornstarch or flour with cold water until completely dissolved. Add this to the gravy, and it should thicken right up.

2. If your sauce is thick and lumpy and you are having a hard time stirring, use a good wire whip and make it easy on yourself.

If after all these directions, you think this is hard, believe me, it isn't. Instead of washing away the makings of a great gravy, add a handful of flour, a little water, and it's magic!

"Chicken" Gravy

Yield: 1¾ to 3½ cups

It's not easy to make chicken gravy when you don't have a chicken. It's even harder if you don't have any tofu or something greasy in the bottom of your skillet to get you started. This is a recipe that is not too fancy, sort of like what Ma Joad made for her family on the way to California. Best when ladled over biscuits, rice, or mashed potatoes, this gravy is good on anything.

This recipe literally brings tears to my eyes. I was weaned on chicken gravy. You'll need:

1 big handful flour *(OK, about ⅓ cup—Use white or whole wheat; the best is a combination of white and chick-pea flour).*
¼ cup nutritional yeast flakes
3 tablespoons soy margarine plus
  2 teaspoons toasted sesame oil
1 to 3 cups warm soymilk, milk, or rice milk, depending on how thick you want your gravy
Several pinches salt
Hard boiled egg, chopped up *(optional)*
¼ teaspoon pepper

Generously cover the bottom of a cast-iron skillet with the flour, and warm over low heat. The secret of this gravy is to let the flour brown very slowly. Stay close at first; you won't have to stir very much. After a few minutes, just stand there and stir away. Add the nutritional yeast now and keep stirring. If the flour should begin to brown too quickly or start to burn, turn the heat down—it's up too high. You want a nice golden brown.

Add the margarine and keep stirring; it should make a paste. Pour in the warm milk or soymilk slowly, and add the salt while continuing to stir. The lumps will go away. By this time, you should stop using a wooden spoon and start using a whip. Now is the time to get any and all of the lumps out. How thick you like your gravy determines how much liquid you pour in. If you want a thinner gravy, use more milk; if not, don't use as much in the beginning. Chop the egg and add it along with lots of freshly grated black pepper. That's it! You can taste it now and see if it needs more salt or a dash of tamari.

PS: If you have just cooked anything in your skillet and there's something left, such as bits and pieces of onions, this the best time to make gravy. Don't let this go to waste—add a handful of flour directly to the skillet and follow my directions.

If you don't eat eggs, then good for you; here's another way to make it. Add ¼ cup sesame seeds to the flour in the beginning, and let it all roast together. Follow the directions from there, and just omit the egg.

Nutritional Yeast Cheese

Yield: 2½ to 3 cups

I got this recipe from The Farm Vegetarian Cookbook. *It is a book I would recommend to anyone who is into trying a meat-free, dairy-free diet. It has lots of good recipes and explains how to make your own soymilk and tofu at home. This is a recipe I don't know what I would do without. You can use it to replace cheese in any Italian dish like lasagne, zucchini Parmesan, or even pizza. It's a good topping for stuffed peppers, hot sandwiches, or just plain with rice or biscuits. I like to steam a whole cauliflower and ladle this sauce over it. It also makes a great base for a casserole.*

When using nutritional yeast be sure you have the right thing. Brewer's yeast and torula yeast do not taste the same. Besides the fact that this is delicious, it has more B vitamins than just about anything else I can think of.

Don't feel like you'll be deprived if you go non-dairy; I have used this in place of cheese successfully every time I have made it. It's the best.

1 cup good-tasting nutritional yeast flakes
⅓ cup flour
1½ teaspoons salt
2 cups water
¼ to ½ cup soy margarine
½ teaspoon garlic powder *(optional)*
2 teaspoons wet mustard *(optional)*

Mix the yeast flakes, flour, and salt together in a pan. Gradually add the water while stirring with a whisk. Make a smooth paste and continue adding the water until it's all used up. Place over medium heat and stir constantly until the sauce starts to thicken and bubble. Let it cook about 30 more seconds. Remove from the heat and stir in the margarine and mustard.

If you want a thicker, stretchier cheese, substitute 3 tablespoons cornstarch and 1 tablespoon flour for the ⅓ cup flour called for. Use ½ cup of oil instead of the margarine, and add as much as 1 cup more water at the end—whatever is needed to make a smooth, pourable sauce.

Wild Woman's Bar-Be-Que Sauce

Yield: about 8 cups

This is the best bar-be-que sauce I've ever had. It's a must for any outdoor to-do. Make a lot because people will come over and ask you for a whole bowl to eat with their dinner.

Don't ever be afraid to alter a recipe to your needs. Once I was making bar-be-que sauce and I had a little bit of baked peaches left over. They had been so good, with brown sugar and cinnamon. I didn't want to throw them away or eat them right then either, so I took a chance and dumped them in the bar-be-que sauce. It was the best bar-be-que sauce I've ever had, and I've never been able to duplicate it. So take a chance—it could be the best thing you ever ate.

3 onions, thinly sliced
2 cloves garlic, smashed and chopped
⅓ cup oil
1 teaspoon allspice
½ teaspoon cayenne
¾ cup molasses
½ cup prepared mustard
2 tablespoons dark miso dissolved in ½ cup water
Two to three 28-ounce cans tomato sauce (depending on how much your pot will hold and how many you are feeding)
2 tablespoons brown sugar or other sweetener
1 teaspoon chili powder
Juice from ½ lemon *(optional)*
1 tablespoon ginger juice *(see end of recipe),* or 2 teaspoons powdered ginger
2 tablespoons tamari
Salt, to taste

Sauté the onions and garlic in the oil; when soft, add the allspice, cayenne, molasses, and mustard. Stir around and cook a few more minutes, then add the rest of the ingredients. Let it simmer a few hours. After it cooks awhile, taste and add more allspice or cayenne if it needs a kick. Maybe a touch more molasses? Add the miso dissolved in water. That's it.

Mario's Hot Sauce

Yield: 4 to 5 cups

A note on grating ginger and ginger juice

Grate ginger on the fine edge of your grater (not the tiniest one though) until you have about a loosely packed ¼ cup.

You can be fancy if you want to and twist this up in a cheese cloth, squeezing out the juice, but I usually just put it in my hand and give it a real hard squeeze. You can squeeze this right over the pot or into a spoon if you want to measure exactly. Fresh ginger juice is the secret ingredient in a lot of my recipes, and the taste simply cannot be duplicated. If you have to use powdered ginger, use 1 to 2 teaspoons.

Another way to do this is by finely grating the ginger and putting it through a garlic press.

If you love ginger, take a 32-ounce bottle of a bland oil, like canola, and heat it gently in a skillet. Add a finely sliced piece of ginger the size of your thumb. Cook over low heat for about 10 minutes or so. Put the oil and ginger back in the bottle. (Remove the ginger after 2 days.) Enjoy in almost anything, especially when making Chinese food.

Mario is a very picky eater. He won't eat a thing unless it has hot sauce on it. He perfected the following recipe, and we both swear by it.

Put a touch of sweetener in the blender with the cukes and peppers if you like your sauce sweet.

1 cucumber
3 to 8 jalapeño peppers *(depending on how hot you like it)*
2 medium green peppers
1 red onion
Two 12-ounce cans tomatoes *(without their juice)*, or 4 to 5 fresh seeded tomatoes
½ cup finely chopped fresh coriander or parsley *(Mario says never substitute dried herbs for this.)*

Blend the cucumber and jalapeños in a blender until you have a very smooth liquid. Chop the green pepper, onion, and tomatoes very finely. Put in a bowl and stir in the cucumber/jalapeño mixture along with the chopped coriander or parsley. Eat this immediately.

Enchilada Sauce

Yield: 5 to 6 cups

A huge pot of beans had been simmering on the stove, oil was popping in a big skillet, and Tommy Merritt had just given me a second wink from across a big bowl of hot sauce.

"The secret is to just pretend you're making Mexican gravy," he said. I watched as he dumped a bunch of onions into the oil. The onions sizzled, he threw in some herbs, and by this time the smell was incredible.

"Yeah, my mamma always let me stir the gravy when I was little," he said, dipping his finger in the sauce and swearing at not being able to get anything hot enough this far from home.

⅓ cup oil
1 to 2 onions, chopped
2 cloves garlic, smashed and chopped
1 tablespoon chili powder
¼ teaspoon cayenne
1 to 2 tablespoons savory
⅓ cup flour
3 cups liquid *(you can use half tomato juice and half bean juice or water)*
Salt and pepper, to taste

Heat the oil in a skillet, add the onions and garlic, and sauté a minute or two, then add the spices and herbs. Let them cook with the onions; it helps bring out their flavor. Add the flour and stir until brown but not burnt. Add more oil or a little soy margarine if you need to to keep the mixture moist. Stir until there are no floury lumps and the onions are soft. Add whatever liquid you are using and the salt, and stir until thickened. Enjoy over any Mexican dish: burritos, enchiladas, rice, quesadillas, or cornbread.

Tomato Gravy

Yield: 5½ cups

Tomatoes and gravy in one? Now that is an unbeatable combination, real good with grits, cornbread or over greens!

3 tablespoons soy margarine
3 tablespoons white flour
½ onion, chopped
1 clove garlic, minced
4 large ripe tomatoes with their juice,
    peeled and chopped
½ cup warm soymilk
1 tablespoon vegetarian broth powder
½ teaspoon sugar
¼ teaspoon pepper
¼ teaspoon salt

Melt the margarine in a skillet over medium heat, add the flour, and let cook a few minutes. Add the onions and garlic, and sauté until tender. Stir in the tomatoes and bring to a boil. Reduce the heat and simmer for about 2 to 3 minutes. Stir in the warm soymilk and remaining ingredients.

Roast "Beef" Gravy

Yield: 1 to 1½ cups

Last year I was lucky enough to spend a week in Paris. While enjoying lunch at some chic bistro, I took a bite of my rice and freaked out. Whatever was on it tasted just like beef gravy. After a long consultation with the waiter (it was long because I didn't know what he was saying, and the only foreign language I know is Spanish), he assured me "No carne!" I'm sure there is some fancy name for this sauce, but I call it roast beef gravy.

3 to 4 tablespoons soy margarine
1 onion, sliced thinly into half moons
¾ to 1½ cups red wine *(must be red)*

Melt the margarine in a skillet. Add the onions; let brown and get very tender. Pour in the wine. Let simmer until the wine has reduced itself by about half. (It should look like a thick onion sauce.) Serve over rice, or as any Southern Frenchman would do, "sop at gravy up wid a big ole hunk of bread."

Southwestern Gravy

Yield: 6½ cups (or 1 large bowl of soup!)

When I was a little girl, our family went to Myrtle Beach every summer. One year the man who rented the umbrella beside us said something I have never forgotten. "I've had the same thing for lunch every day for the last 12 years; a cantaloupe, a bowl of gravy, and a Pepsi."

This statement has puzzled me since the day I heard it. What kind of gravy? Did he pour it in the cantaloupe or have it on the side? Did he eat them together or one at a time? Did the Pepsi have to be in a glass or was a bottle O.K.?

I always imagined he had this kind of gravy, as it is good enough to eat right out of the bowl.

¼ cup flour
¼ cup vegetable oil
2 onions, chopped
2 cups hot water
One 14½-ounce can diced tomatoes, undrained
One 8-ounce can diced tomatoes and green chiles
One 6-ounce can tomato paste
1 teaspoon Pick-a-Peppa Sauce
3 tablespoons vegetable broth powder or cubes
¼ teaspoon each sugar, salt, and pepper

Whisk together the flour and vegetable oil in a skillet over low heat. Stir almost constantly until the mixture is caramel-colored, about 10 minutes. (It should be darker than golden brown.) Add the onion and continue stirring about 5 more minutes. Stir in the hot water and bring to a boil. Add the remaining ingredients, reduce the heat, and simmer for 5 minutes. Serve with grits, tofu scramble, greens, black-eyed peas, or anything Southern (except cantaloupe, that is . . .)

Pies

Small cheer and great welcome makes a merry feast.
William Shakespeare, 1564-1616

A little peace in an orchard grew—
A little peach of emerald hue;
Warmed by the sun and wet by the dew,
It grew.

Eugene Field

Hints About Pie Making

There is something about the mystique of a good pie that fascinates me. The picture of a little house with a thatched roof and rose garden is just not complete without a couple of pies cooling on the window sill.

Loretta Lynn had won 18 (or was it 22?) blue ribbons for her pies at the county fair before she ever had a gold record. Marybelle Morgan has already compiled the statistics: Ask any American man what he wants for dessert and he'll say pie 80% of the time. If he's white, he'll more than likely say apple, and if he's black, he'll probably say sweet potato. And remember, pies aren't just for dessert; there's quiche, pizza, vegetable pie, and deep-dish country pie, to name a few.

The recipe hardly ever varies, but ask any cook and she'll say, "Now there's a trick to it . . ." And of course, no trick is ever the same. I nearly drove myself crazy trying to make the perfect pie crust. If you can master the crust, the filling is a cinch. Here is every secret and trick I've ever heard of or come up with myself:

1. If you are making a traditional pie crust, start off on the right foot and use whole wheat pastry flour. The gluten content is much lower—that's what makes it pastry flour. Gluten is what makes the dough all sticky and gooey, like what happens when you make bread, not pie crust.

2. It is my personal opinion that any shortening that is consumed by me goes directly to my thigh in the form of a big lump of cellulite. (And remains there forever!) You might be asking yourself what this has to do with pie crust. Well, in my experimenting, a lot of real heavy-duty pie makers told me to use Crisco to get a perfect pie crust. In my relentless search, I admit, I tried it. The pie was good, great even, but as I was cleaning up, something very strange happened. I had heard that a food processor worked well for making pie crust, instead of cutting the shortening in by hand. While washing the dishes, I noticed there was a big blob of shortening stuck in the cylinder opening on the lid of the machine. I couldn't reach it with my hand so I figured I would just melt it off with real hot water. I held that thing under the steaming hot water for almost ten minutes and couldn't believe my eyes. It was the immovable force—no wonder my thighs looked the way they did. After

78

stabbing it with a long, skinny knife, I finally loosened its grip.

Use whatever you want: soy margarine or any oil. They all work more or less the same, but don't say I didn't warn you.

3. The one thing that all cooks agree on is this: Handle the pastry as little as possible. This includes stirring and rolling it out.

4. When you are rolling out the pastry, do it between 2 sheets of waxed paper. It will keep the dough from sticking to the table, and you can just pick the whole thing up and flip it right into the pie plate. Also, when you do this, put a couple of drops of water under the waxed paper to keep it from slipping around while you're trying to roll.

5. The first couple of times I made pies, I would get real excited right after I got the dough in the plate and pinch the sides of the crust into fancy designs. Then after I got the filling in and the top layer of crust on, I would realize, "Wait a minute, you aren't supposed to pinch the sides until last, so you can pinch the top and bottom together." (Don't make that dumb mistake!)

6. Always make sure you use ice water. It helps make the pastry flaky by keeping the fat from melting into the flour.

7. Remember to preheat your oven; start your pie in a very hot oven (400°F to 425°F), and turn it down after about 15 minutes. The cold dough in a hot oven makes the dough puff into a very light, flaky pastry, and that is what you are after.

8. If you aren't going to use your dough right away, refrigerate it. (It's best to chill at least 1 hour anyway.) If you leave it in the fridge a long time, let it sit out about 1 hour before you try to roll it out.

9. When you put the filling in a pie, don't be afraid to heap it in—it will cook down a bit.

10. If you are baking a pie crust by itself, don't forget to prick the bottom. If the air can't escape, it will make a bubble in the crust.

11. Some people say you should brush the bottom of your crust with egg white or milk so it won't get soggy. I never have milk or eggs around, so I use soymilk or egg replacer; both work fine. I only do this with real juicy pies like blueberry or cherry.

Aunt Sally Dyer's Basic Pie Crust

Yield: One 9-inch pie with a top and bottom crust or 2 shells.

2 cups whole wheat pastry flour
1 teaspoon salt
⅔ cup soy margarine
No more than 5 tablespoons ice water

Stir the flour and salt together in a bowl. Cut in the margarine with a pastry cutter, 2 knives cutting against each other, or even the tips of your fingers until the pastry is somewhere between the texture of cornmeal and peas. Barely sprinkle the dough with ice water. Don't put it all in at once, just a few spoonfuls at a time. Stir it quickly with a fork; as soon as you can make it hold together in a ball, it's done.

You can roll it out now, but it's best to refrigerate it for an hour ar so. (It can be left in the fridge for about a week if covered tightly in plastic.) When you are ready to roll it out, divide the dough into 2 pieces, and roll between 2 pieces of wax paper. (A few drops of water on your counter will keep the wax paper from slipping.) Try not to use much more flour. Roll from the center of the dough outward. Pull off the top sheet of paper, and turn the crust into a pie plate, pressing it lightly into the bottom. Now the pie is ready to be filled. You can make a lattice crust by cutting out thin strips and weaving them over the filling, or roll out a top crust to place over the entire pie. Cut a little design in the top if you'd like, or just prick it with a fork.

If the crust is to be baked unfilled, flute the edge and either prick the bottom with a fork or put in a handful of dry beans. Bake at 425°F for 12 to 15 minutes, or until light brown.

Ginger Snap Crust

Yield: One 8 or 9-inch pie crust

This is easy, I know, but I included it so you'd have it at your fingertips whenever you needed it. This is great for cream-style pies or something like spicy peach or pear pie.

1½ cups crushed ginger snaps (about 26 cookies)
2 tablespoons sugar
⅓ cup melted soy margarine

Stir together all the ingredients, and press the mixture into the bottom and sides of an 8 or 9-inch pie plate. Bake at 350°F for 8 to 10 minutes. Cool on a rack.

Pumpkin Pie with an Oat Crust

Yield: One 9-inch pie (6 to 8 servings)

This pie is incredible and so much better made with fresh pumpkin instead of canned pumpkin. You can vary it by using cooked butternut, buttercup, or acorn squash.

4 cups peeled fresh pumpkin chunks

1 cup apple juice

⅓ cup maple syrup plus 2 tablespoons molasses or brown sugar

½ teaspoon salt

1 teaspoon cinnamon

½ teaspoon powdered ginger,
   or 1 teaspoon fresh ginger juice
   (See p. 73.)

Pinch of cloves or allspice

Egg replacer equal to 3 eggs

1 teaspoon vanilla

½ cup chopped pecans, English walnuts, or black walnuts

Simmer the pumpkin chunks in the apple juice until soft. Mash briefly with the rest of the ingredients in a medium bowl, and process in batches in a blender or food processor until very smooth. If it seems like it needs to be a little firmer, add another portion of egg replacer. Pour into a 9-inch pie shell, and sprinkle the top generously with chopped nuts. Bake at 350°F for 25 to 30 minutes. Let sit awhile before cutting into slices.

Eleanor Dare's Mincemeat Pie

Yield: One 9-inch pie (6 to 8 servings)

Who's Eleanor Dare? The first European woman to give birth in America—to a girl named Virginia.

3 heaping tablespoons dark miso
1 cup apple cider
1 cup raisins
1 cup currants
2 cups chopped pineapple
½ cup honey or maple syrup
1 cup molasses
1 to 2 tablespoons grated orange peel
1 to 2 tablespoons grated lemon peel
3 cups chopped apples
1 teaspoon ground cloves
1 teaspoon cinnamon
1 teaspoon nutmeg
Pinch of salt
Juice of 1 orange
Juice of 1 lemon
½ cup chopped walnuts *(optional)*
½ to 1 cup brandy *(optional)*

Dissolve the miso in the apple cider before adding. Mix with all the other ingredients in a pot, except the brandy (if using), and simmer over medium heat. If this seems really watery or runny, dissolve a couple of tablespoons of kudzu or cornstarch in cold water, add to the mincemeat mixture, and stir until thickened.

You might want this to mellow in the fridge for a couple of days. Spoon into a 9-inch unbaked pie shell. Make a lattice crust for the top. (See general hints for making pie crust, pages 78-79.) Bake at 350°F for about 35 minutes, or until the crust is done.

Margot Channing's Pecan Pie

Yield: One 9-inch pie (6 to 8 servings)

Only one thing in the world tastes better than chocolate, and that's pecan pie. This is a delicious and easy recipe. And remember Margot's famous advice when you make this is—fasten your seatbelt, it's going to be a bumpy ride.

Egg replacer equal to 3 eggs
1 cup dark corn syrup
¾ cup sugar
⅓ cup very soft or melted soy margarine
Pinch salt
1 teaspoon vanilla extract
½ cup chopped pecans
One 9-inch pie crust
1 cup pecan halves

Beat the egg replacer, corn syrup, sugar, margarine, and salt until smooth. Stir in the chopped pecans. Pour into the unbaked pie crust, and arrange the pecan halves on top. Bake at 350°F for 40 to 50 minutes, or until set.

Sweet Potato Pie

Yield: One 9-inch pie (6 to 8 servings)

¼ cup soy margarine
¾ cup honey, or ¼ cup maple syrup and ½ cup barley malt
1 tablespoon molasses
1½ cups squash or sweet potatoes
1 cup cold water
2 tablespoons kudzu or cornstarch
¾ teaspoon ginger
Pinch of cinnamon
Pinch of salt
1½ cups chopped pecans
1 teaspoon vanilla

Preheat the oven to 350°F. Cream the margarine and the sweetener and molasses. Puree the squash in a blender, and in a separate bowl, mix the water and kudzu. When this is dissolved, add it to the stuff in the blender. Add the ginger, cinnamon, and salt. Stir this into the margarine and honey mix and then add the pecans and vanilla. Pour into an unbaked pie shell, and bake at for 40 to 45 minutes until done.

Nanny Jackson's Sweet Potato Pie

Yield: Two 9-inch pies (12 to 16 servings)

Old fashioned, old timey, nothing modern here (and nothing you'll miss, either).

2 cups peeled sweet potato chunks,
    boiled and mashed
1 teaspoon nutmeg
1 teaspoon cinnamon
1 teaspoon ground cloves
1 teaspoon ginger powder
1½ cups sugar
Egg replacer equal to 4 eggs
3 cups plain or sweetened soymilk
2 unbaked 9-inch pie shells
Pecan halves for topping *(optional)*

Stir together all the filling ingredients, except the milk, until smooth. Add the milk and stir well again. Pour into the unbaked pie shells, and bake at 350°F for about 45 minutes. Shake very gently to test for doneness; they should be firm and not still liquidy. If you really like pecans, you can arrange pecan halves over the top of the pies before baking.

The Knockout Punch Chocolate No-Cream Pie

Yield: One 9-inch pie (6 to 8 servings)

This is completely delicious and unbeatable as a pie or pudding. A really good crust to use with this pie is whole grain graham crackers. (There are good ones on the market which contain no sugar or lard.) Crush a couple of packages, and mix with ½ cup melted soy margarine. Press into a pie plate. Carob lovers can substitute carob for the cocoa in this.

⅓ cup unsweetened cocoa
⅓ cup cornstarch or arrowroot
½ teaspoon salt
1 teaspoon instant espresso, or
    1 tablespoon instant coffee
3 cups soymilk or coconut milk
¾ cup honey or other liquid sweetener
1 teaspoon vanilla
1 tablespoon Kahlua, or ½ teaspoon rum
    extract
1 prebaked 9-inch pie shell *(with ½ cup unsweetened grated coconut added to the dough while combining the flour and salt)*

In a saucepan, stir the cocoa, cornstarch, salt, and instant coffee together. Stir in the soymilk and honey over low heat. Let come to a boil and continue to cook about 10 minutes. Stir in the vanilla and kahlua or rum. Pour this into the pie shell, and let cool.

Berry Pie

Yield: One 9-inch pie (6 to 8 servings)

My great-grandmother Jenny Hunter was a true Southern matriarch. She lived to be 99 and still had all her teeth, and her mind was as sharp as a tack. There are many family stories about her— this is one of my favorites.

It was a beautiful summer day in July of 1892. The Baptist Church was having a picnic and bake sale. Jenny had made several cakes (coconut was her specialty) and three or four pies to donate to the sale. The family, cakes, and pies, were loaded into the buggy pulled by Butterfly and Grasshopper, the pet ponies. Maybe there were more ruts and bumps in the road than usual, maybe it was a hot day, but when they arrived at the picnic, the cakes and pies were in pretty bad shape.

Although still delicious, Jenny's pies were worse for the wear. She took matters into her own hands when it came time to auction her baked goods. She took a pie, climbed on a chair, held her pie aloft and declared, "Slightly disfigured, but still in the ring!"

Anytime anyone in my family makes something that doesn't come out of the pan quite right or has torn-up a little, someone will always make this comment, which I consider a big compliment.

4 to 5 cups berries *(blackberry, blueberry, red raspberry, strawberry, huckleberry, or cherries with all the pits removed)*
1 tablespoon cornstarch, tapioca, or kudzu
¼ to ½ cup sugar, depending on sweetness of the berries
1 tablespoon lemon juice *(optional)*
Top and bottom crust for a 9-inch pie
2 to 3 tablespoons soy margarine

Wash and pick through the berries, slicing them up if they are large. Reserve a bit of the juice that results from slicing the berries, and dissolve the cornstarch or kudzu into it. Add this back to the berries, along with the sugar and lemon juice. Toss and let sit 10 minutes. (At this point you could also add a handful of raisins, a bit of applesauce, or any spice you particularly like: cinnamon, anise, or cardamom). Pour out into an unbaked pie shell, and dot with the margarine. Cover with the other pastry crust or a lattice top.

Start this in a hot oven (425°F to 450°F) for about 10 minutes, then turn the heat down and finish baking at about 350°F for about 40 minutes. The crust should be brown and beautiful.

Tofu Pot Pie with Cornmeal Crust

Yield: 8 servings

The crust can be chilling while you do the rest of the pie. If you don't know how to make a pie crust, read a bit about it on pages 78-79 before you get started here. When I make this, I usually make a fancy criss-cross lattice top crust, and leave it at that. If you want a bottom crust also, just double the crust recipe.

Pastry crust:

¾ cup whole wheat pastry flour
½ cup cornmeal
⅓ cup soy margarine or sesame oil
3 tablespoons cold water

Filling:

⅓ cup oil
1 pound tofu, cubed
⅓ cup flour, any kind
Dash each paprika, salt, and pepper
1 onion, chopped
2 tablespoons miso
¾ cup water
2 carrots, thinly sliced
1 potato, cooked and diced
½ cup sliced mushrooms
Tamari, to taste
¼ cup sliced toasted almonds *(optional)*

To make the pasty crust, mix the dry ingredients together, then cut in the margarine or oil. Stir while adding the cold water until the dough leaves the sides of the bowl. Wrap the dough in waxed paper until you're ready to roll it out.

To make the filling, heat the oil in a skillet. When it's hot, add the flour, paprika, salt, pepper, and onion. Give it a good stir, and turn down the heat. Dissolve the miso in the water, and add to the skillet, stirring until slightly thickened. Then add the chopped carrots and potato, sliced mushrooms, tamari, and almonds, if using. Spoon into a 9 x 13-inch casserole dish with or without a bottom crust.

Roll out a top crust, and cut into long strips. Lay it criss-cross over the pie. Bake at 375°F for about 45 minutes, or until the crust is brown and the filling is bubbling.

Nolichucky Vegetable Pie with Nut Crust

Yield: One 9-inch pie (6 to 8 servings)

If your cupboard is bare and you're having a down-home dinner, go ahead and use the potatoes as listed in this recipe. If you're putting on the dog, use marinated artichoke hearts or cooked fresh broccoli or asparagus instead. This crust is equally good with fruit pies or chocolate no-cream pie; just toss in a tablespoon of honey with the crumbs before pressing into the pie plate.

Nut crust:

2 cups crushed nuts *(any combination of sesame seeds, cashews, pecans, walnuts, brazil nuts, almonds, pumpkin seeds, filberts, peanuts, or sunflower seeds)*
1 tablespoon of pastry flour
1 to 2 teaspoons sesame oil *(optional)*

Slightly roast the nuts or seeds in a dry skillet (not too much because they'll cook again with the pie). Grind in a blender or food processor until about like crumbs. Pour into an 8 or 9-inch pie plate. Toss with the flour and some or all of the oil (only if it seems dry). Press into the bottom and sides of the pie plate.

Filling:

1 to 1½ cups sliced mushrooms
1 onion, chopped
½ cabbage, finely chopped
1 to 2 boiled potatoes, cut into small pieces
½ cup finely chopped parsley
1 clove garlic, finely chopped
1 to 2 hard boiled eggs *(optional)*
1½ to 2 cups of your favorite creamy sauce
  (it can be a non-dairy "cheese" sauce, dill sauce, mustard sauce, onion sesame sauce, cheese sauce, or whatever you like)
Salt, pepper, and tamari, to taste

Preheat the oven to 350°F. Sauté the mushrooms, onions, and cabbage until just soft, but not cooked all the way through. Remove from the heat and stir in the chopped, cooled potatoes (or other cooked vegetables, if you're using them), and parsley. Pour this mixture into your uncooked pie crust. If you're using eggs, slice them over the top of the pie. Pour a little of the sauce over the pie, not enough to be soggy, but enough so the vegetables won't dry out. If you have any sauce leftover, that's OK. (People usually ask for some to pour over their pie like gravy.) Bake for 30 to 40 minutes or until bubbling.

Captain's Country Pie with Biscuit Crust

Yield: 6 to 8 servings

2 to 3 tablespoons sesame seeds

3 to 4 tablespoons olive oil

1 large onion, chopped

1 pound frozen tofu, thawed, and squeezed dry

3 tablespoons good-tasting nutritional yeast flakes

Tamari, to taste

1 cup small whole mushrooms

2 cups corn kernels

1½ tablespoons cornstarch dissolved in ⅓ to ½ cup cold water

1 recipe Baking Powder Biscuits, p. 38

Lightly roast the sesame seeds in a dry skillet. Add the oil and onion, and let cook a few minutes, then crumble in the tofu. Shake in the nutritional yeast, and drizzle the tamari over the top. Let cook until it's brown all over and smells real good. Add the mushrooms and let brown until they're cooked about half way through. Stir in the corn kernels last, and remove from the heat. If the mixture is very dry, add the dissolved cornstarch. The exact amount of water to mix it with here is always different as you will never be quite sure how moist the vegetables will be. Spoon the mixture into a 9 x 13-inch casserole dish.

Preheat your oven to 400°F to 425°F. Make a biscuit dough according to the recipe. If you want, when you make this you can add a little chopped parsley, onion, poppy seeds, sesame seeds, even cheese to the dry ingredients before adding the liquid. Roll out the dough as for biscuits. Cut out large biscuits and lay on top of the casserole, or you can lay the whole dough over the top.

Bake the casserole for about 20 to 25 minutes. The top should look just like regular biscuits, nice and brown. If you lift the biscuit layer up with a fork, it should be wet from the sauce, but not doughy. Serve at once with mashed potatoes, gravy, and some greens.

Main Courses

*Show me another pleasure like dinner which comes
every day and lasts an hour.*

Talleyrand 1754-1838

Low Country Boil

Yield: 6 servings

This begs for a nice hot bread of any kind and nothing more.

1 tablespoon olive oil or toasted sesame oil
2 onions, cut into quarters
1 to 2 green bell peppers
Seven to ten 1-inch cubes seitan
3 to 4 tablespoons tamari
4 potatoes, cut into quarters
2 turnips, cut into chunks
1 small cabbage, cut into quarters or fifths
1 tablespoon Old Bay Seasoning
1 hot pepper *(Depending on how hot you like your food, use anything from a habañero to a sweet banana pepper, finely chopped.)*
½ cup chopped fresh parsley
¼ teaspoon each salt and pepper
2 ears corn on the cob

Pour the oil in the bottom of a Dutch oven or a big soup pot. Let it get hot, then add the onions and peppers. When the onions are transparent, add the seitan. Drizzle a little of the tamari over it. Continue to cook a few minutes, then add the potatoes, turnips, and cabbage. Add the remaining ingredients (except the corn on the cob) and about 2 cups water, enough to keep the vegetables from sticking, but not enough to make it be like soup. Cover and simmer about 1½ to 2 hours. Use a heat diffuser over your stovetop burner, if necessary, and also add small amounts of water if too much evaporation is occurring.

Break the ears of corn into 2 or 3 pieces, and add to the pot the last hour of cooking time. Serve in a soup bowl.

Pocahontas Stuffed Pumpkin

Yield: 8 to 10 servings

I love to make this for a big Thanksgiving or Christmas dinner, but most stores stop carrying pumpkins after Halloween. This October, buy two pumpkins, carve one, and keep the other one for a big dinner. It's also nice to get small pumpkins for individual servings of this.

1 medium pumpkin *(Make sure it will fit into your oven.)*
⅔ cup oil
⅓ cup tamari
1 tablespoon grated ginger
3 onions, sliced into crescents
4 stalks celery, chopped
1 heaping tablespoon sage *(You really can't use too much of this, so don't worry about going overboard.)*
2 teaspoons thyme
2 cups bread crumbs
2 cups any leftover cooked grain *(Rice works great.)*
¼ cup toasted sunflower seeds
¼ cup finely chopped fresh parsley
½ cup melted soy margarine *(optional)*
Lots of freshly grated ginger

Salt, to taste

Cut out the top of the pumpkin, and set it aside. Scrape out the stringy pulp and seeds. Make a marinade by combining the oil, tamari, and 1 tablespoon grated ginger. Prick the inside of the pumpkin all over with a fork, and pour in the marinade. Turn it all around so that the pumpkin walls get covered.

Preheat the oven to 400°F. Sauté the onion and celery, and when about half done, add the sage and thyme and cook until you can smell the herbs. It won't take long. Remove from the heat and combine in a big bowl with the rest of the ingredients. If the mixture seems dry, add the melted margarine; if not, you can omit it. Stuff the mixture into your pumpkin, and put the top back on. Sit this in a baking dish or a pie plate, and bake for about 1 hour, or until the pumpkin is soft.

Serve this immediately, encouraging your guests to take pumpkin along with the stuffing. People get so caught up in the stuffing, they forget that the pumpkin is part of the dinner also, not just a container.

Coal Miner's "Chicken-Fried" Steak & Gravy

Yield: 6 to 8 servings

O.K. It's not exactly like chicken, but that also depends on how healthy you want to be. For a real artery-buster, you can make smaller chicken-style nuggets and deep-fry them, then serve them with gravy. Or take the healthy route, make patties, and bake them in the oven. I usually make medium-size patties and fry them in a few tablespoons of oil in an electric non-stick skillet. However you make this, it's a great burger recipe. You can substitute tofu or breadcrumbs if you don't have enough chick-peas or if you don't like oats, etc.

"Steaks":
1 small or medium onion
2 cloves garlic
2 cups cooked chick-peas, or 1 cup chick-peas plus 1 cup tofu *(Save the liquid from the chick-peas, and set aside.)*
¼ cup tahini
2 tablespoons Dijon mustard
1 teaspoon vegetable broth seasoning *(optional)*
¾ to 1 cup quick or rolled oats

Breading mix:
⅓ cup good-tasting nutritional yeast flakes
⅓ cup flour
⅓ cup sesame seeds

⅓ cup oil *(if you are frying these)*

Gravy:
Leftover breading mixture *(about ⅓ cup)*
Leftover chick-pea water plus soymilk, enough to measure 3 cups
4 tablespoons soy margarine
1 teaspoon salt
Pinch black pepper
Dash tamari

This is a recipe for the food processor. If you don't have one, use your hands and mash all the ingredients together well. Cut the onion into chunks and process first with the garlic, then add the chick-peas and the rest of the ingredients, leaving the oats for last. Test now to see if the mixture will hold together, adding more oats if necessary.

Shape into patties, balls, or nuggets. Dredge in the breading mix, and fry in the oil or bake until browned on both sides and crispy.

To make gravy, if you fried your "steaks," use whatever oil is left in the skillet from frying the chicken-fried steak. Add whatever you have left of the breading mixture to the skillet. Let toast a minute or two, then add the margarine, melt, and let cook over low heat a few minutes more until slightly brown but not burned. Add the leftover chick-pea liquid and soymilk. Mix well and cook over low heat. Keep your eye on it and stir after a few minutes. Keep stirring until it gets as thick as you want it. Add salt, pepper, and tamari. Serve over "chicken-fried steak" with a salad or biscuits, depending, of course, on how healthy you want to be.

Tofu Scrambled Eggs

Yield: 3 to 4 servings

This is incredible with biscuits and gravy, soy sausage, or pancakes. But why wait and have it for breakfast?

1 cup chopped onions
1 clove garlic, chopped
¼ to ½ cup mushrooms
½ cup finely chopped green and red bell peppers
¼ cup oil
¼ teaspoon turmeric *(optional—if you want yellow color)*
2 teaspoons thyme
Dash of cayenne or Tabasco sauce *(if you like things hot or a little spicier)*
½ cup good-tasting nutritional yeast flakes
1 pound tofu, well drained
2 tablespoons poppy seeds
Salt, pepper, and parsley, to taste

Sauté the onions, garlic, mushrooms, and peppers in the oil in that order. Add the spices and nutritional yeast, lower the heat, and cook a few more minutes. Crumble in the tofu, and add the salt, pepper, and parsley. Let simmer 10 minutes or so. If you think it needs a little more yellow coloring, add more turmeric, but remember that the color comes out slowly so don't put in too much.

93

Tofu "Fish" Sandwiches with Tartar Sauce

Yield: 6 sandwiches

These sandwiches are a little different from real fish sandwiches, but the cornmeal and tartar sauce makes them good sandwiches whether they taste exactly like fish or not!

Marinade:

¼ cup tamari mixed with ¼ cup water
2 teaspoons kelp powder
1 teaspoon dry mustard
1 clove garlic, pressed
¼ cup olive oil
Good squeeze of lemon juice

1 pound tofu, sliced into 6 pieces
½ cup cornmeal
½ to ⅔ cup oil
6 buns
Lettuce, tomato slices, and tartar sauce, for topping (*Use your own tartar sauce or use the recipe on this page.*)

Mix the marinade ingredients and add the tofu slices. Marinate at least 2 hours.

Spread the cornmeal on a plate, and coat both sides of the tofu slices generously. Pour ¼ to ⅓ cup of the oil in a skillet. When hot, add the tofu slices. Fry until crispy and golden brown, then turn over and add the remaining oil. When brown on both sides, serve on buns with tomato, lettuce, and lots of tartar sauce.

Tartar Sauce

Yield: about 1½ cups

This keeps really well covered in the fridge.

1 cup mayonnaise
2 teaspoons Dijon mustard
3 tablespoons drained sweet relish or sweet pickle
1 tablespoon grated onion
¼ cup chopped red pepper
Juice of ½ small lemon or 1 lime

Mix all the ingredients together, and enjoy with sandwiches.

Jambalaya

Yield: 8 servings

Just the name jambalaya conjures up mystery. I see mammoth cast-iron kettles with flames licking up the sides and tropical, leafy pathways with secret nooks and fortune tellers. Jambalaya sounds like a secret elixir, as if you had to go to the local voodoo shop for the recipe. I always felt that Blanche DuBois could have held onto her sanity if she could have had just one more good bowl of jambalaya.

½ cup olive oil
3 cups chopped onions
2 cloves garlic
2 bell peppers, chopped
2 small yellow squash, chopped
3 medium tomatoes, peeled and chopped
3 teaspoons salt
1¼ teaspoons cayenne
6 to 8 pieces of your favorite vegetarian
    sausage, thawed and cut into ½-inch
    slices
Flavored seitan, cut in chunks *(optional)*
2 bay leaves
3 cups long grain rice
1 to 2 umeboshi plums, without pits *(to take
    the place of salt pork)*
6 cups water
½ to 1 cup chopped green onion

Heat the oil in a large, heavy pot or cast-iron Dutch oven. Add the onion, garlic, bell pepper, squash, and tomatoes, and half the salt and cayenne. Stir and let the vegetables brown for about 20 minutes. They will be a nice caramel color. Add the vegetarian sausage and seitan, if using, and let brown, stirring occasionally to keep from sticking. Add the bay leaves, rice, remaining salt and pepper, and the umeboshi plums. Let cook a few more minutes. Then add the water, stir, and cover. Let cook 35 minutes, or until all the liquid is absorbed.

I'm telling you right now, young lady or young man, if you dare to lift that lid even once during the first 35 minutes the rice is cooking, I'm going to come over there and give you a piece of my mind. Is that clear?

Remove from the heat and let sit a few minutes. Top with the chopped green onions, and serve.

Big Trouble Tofu

Yield: 2 to 3 servings

*My friend Michelle brought me some tofu one day and said, "This is the best thing you'll ever put into your mouth." She was right. Besides fried-chicken tofu, this is the best tofu I've ever had. But there is a reason I named it big trouble tofu. If you've read through my recipes, you'll find most of them are pretty easy, don't take too long, or have a lot of steps; that's the way I like to cook. This recipe ends all that. It takes forever and is **Big Trouble**, but is all worth it.*

The health food store stopped making tofu this way (probably because it's so much trouble), but Michelle and I could not face life without it, so we've worked over a year to figure out how to do it and make it perfect. Here's how we do it.

2 pieces fresh ginger a little bit bigger than your thumb* *(Pretend you hit your thumb with a hammer—that size. It's better here to use too much rather than too little if you're not sure.)*

1½ to 2 cups strong sweetened ginger tea, steeped all day or overnight

½ cup tamari

¼ cup maple syrup or honey *(Michelle uses maple syrup—I use honey)*

1 lime or ½ lemon *(Michelle uses lime— I use lemon)*

1 clove garlic, crushed

1 tablespoon horseradish

1 tablespoon Dijon mustard

⅛ teaspoon cayenne pepper

Freshly ground black pepper, to taste

1 pound firm tofu

⅓ cup orange juice (optional)

*I have used 2 tablespoons powdered ginger here when I was experimenting, but it is not as good. If you don't have quite enough fresh ginger and need to use some powdered, you can, but try not to use all powder.

To make ginger juice from the ginger, carefully cut off the outer skin and grate the pieces on a grater over a bowl. (See p. 73 for more on how to do this.) To the same bowl add the rest of the ingredients, except the tofu. Stir well to mix everything, including the honey or syrup, which will tend to stay on the bottom until you add it to the tofu. This will be your marinade.

Slice the tofu about ½ inch thick. (Thick slices are important to make it come out right.) Arrange the slices in a baking dish or bowl just the right size so when you pour the marinade over the tofu, it will cover the slices completely. (If you need a little more marinade, you can add equal parts water and tamari to stretch it a little, or just use more ginger tea.) Cover the bowl and let sit in the refrigerator for at least 6 hours or overnight. Next day, remove the tofu from the marinade, but DO NOT throw the marinade out. You'll need it again later.

Preheat the oven to 250°F. Arrange the tofu on a baking sheet. Grind black pepper over the slices, and bake for 20 minutes. Flip the tofu, grind more pepper over it, and bake again for 20 minutes. Remove from the oven and return to the marinade to steep for another 6 hours. (It's important that the tofu start marinating while it's hot.) Bake the tofu again as above, 20 minutes on each side, but don't brush on any of the marinade—it needs to cook dry. (Strain the marinade and save to use on seitan or textured soy chunks—it's too good to throw out.) After this step, you are finally done. Let it come to room temperature or chill. My husband and I think this is better cold than hot. Just another step in the many processes it has already taken to make this.

Can you believe how long it takes? I have tried to leave out steps, but it doesn't taste as good. If you can work out a recipe that tastes as good and is easier, please let me know.

Lame Dog Stew

Yield: 6 to 8 servings

This sounds like a very plain stew. Maybe that's why it's so good.

2 cloves garlic
3 potatoes, cut into big chunks
3 to 4 carrots, cut lengthwise
2 turnips, cut into chunks
4 red radishes, left whole
½ winter squash, peeled and chunked
1 pound tofu, tempeh, or seitan, marinated
  and cut into cubes
1 to 2 tablespoons miso, or 1 vegetable
  broth cube dissolved in 1 cup cold water
3 tablespoons flour dissolved in ½ cup
  cold water
Salt, pepper, tamari, and soy margarine,
  to taste

Pick out a 3 to 4-quart casserole dish to use; it's got to have a good lid. If you don't have one, use an oven-proof bowl and aluminum foil.

Preheat the oven to 350°F. Crush the garlic and rub it all over the bottom and side of the baking dish. Arrange the vegetable and tofu chunks in the dish. Pour the dissolved miso or broth cube and flour over the veggies, and add salt, pepper, tamari, and a few dots of margarine. Cover and bake for 1 hour or until the veggies are done; 15 extra minutes never hurts.

Enchiladas

Yield: 8 servings

This recipe is involved, but it's worth it. I try to make enough for two meals. Once I get all the stuff out and get going, it's just as easy to fill up two casserole dishes as it is one. If you're in a hurry, low on oil, or just trying to cut out some fat from your diet, you can skip frying the tortillas in oil; just roll them up plain.

¼ to ½ cup oil *(or as needed)*
10 to 12 corn tortillas
1 copy of *The Rocky Mountain News (My friend Tommy Merritt says this paper works the best, but I guess any will do.)*
¼ cup tamari
1 to 2 tablespoons vegetarian Worcestershire or Pick-a-Peppa sauce
2 to 3 teaspoons cumin powder
1 teaspoon chili powder
1 pound frozen tofu, thawed and squeezed dry
1 onion, chopped
1 green pepper, chopped
2 cloves garlic
1 cup chopped black olives
1 batch Tommy Merritt's Enchilada Sauce, p. 74
1 cup Nutritional Yeast Cheese, p. 71

Heat the oil in a skillet, and put the tortillas in gently one at a time, frying just a few seconds on each side. Lay between the pages of a newspaper or a brown paper sack (bag, to you Yankees) to absorb the oil.

Make a marinade by mixing the tamari, Worcestershire or Pick-a-Peppa, cumin, and chili powder, and add enough water to make half a cup. Crumble the thawed frozen tofu into a bowl, then pour the marinade over it.

Heat a little more oil in the skillet, and add the chopped onion and green pepper. When half done, add the marinated tofu and sauté until brown. Stir in the olives.

Preheat the oven to 375°F. Place a few spoonfuls of the enchilada sauce on the bottom of a 9 x 13-inch casserole dish before putting the tortillas in so they won't stick. Place a large spoonful of the tofu mixture into a tortilla. Roll it up and place it rolled side down in the casserole dish. Cover the dish with filled tortillas, placed very close together. Then cover the whole thing generously with enchilada sauce and yeast cheese.

Bake for 45 minutes or until very bubbly. Enjoy pronto with any number of things—yellow rice, guacamole—or just by themselves. There are all kinds of things you can stuff the enchiladas with besides what I've mentioned here: beans, tempeh, vegetables, and/or cheese.

Soups

Too many cooks may spoil the broth, but it only takes one to burn it

Madeline Bingham

Close to the back step of one cabin, she found a short row of radishes and hunger assaulted her suddenly. A spicy, sharp-tasting radish was exactly what her stomach craved. Hardly waiting to rub the dirt off on her skirt, she bit off half and swallowed it hastily. It was old and coarse and so peppery that tears started in her eyes.

Margaret Mitchell

Washing Dishes

I suppose everyone has their little quirks, and I confess mine are ironing and washing dishes. Yep, that's right. I love to do the two most hated household chores. I admit I get a thrill from starching the skirt of a cotton house dress. I love it when we stay in hotels that have ironing boards in the room. I can sit happily for hours ironing hankies and silk scarves, content to see the sky-scrapers from my window, through the steam puffing from my iron. Of course, in today's world I don't iron much, there's no need to.

But dishes are a different story altogether. Dishes have to get washed, they need to be done. And did you notice, no matter how much time you stand at the sink washing them, they never seem to be finished? As soon as you get the last batch washed, next time you walk by the sink, there's a dirty teacup, or a spoon, or the remnants of toast, and then there they go again, just piling up. It's so hard to get inspired and going on supper when last night's dishes are stacked in the sink.

Oh, but what about the dishwasher, you'll ask? Not for me. If I'm too lazy to wash them, then I don't deserve to eat off them. No scientist could ever convince me that a machine can get the dishes cleaner than I can.

People say, "I don't cook because I hate washing dishes." I say, "Get better dishes!" All my dishes are different, all styles and colors, from the good Haviland to Fiesta Ware to Homer Laughlin. I like to use lots of them too, gravy boats, serving bowls, water pitchers. Bring on the butter dishes!! It is a joy to look at them. Actually, when I'm washing them is the only time I'm ever really looking at them without food on them. Could you ever get tired of looking at a Blue Willow plate?

Maybe you are lucky enough to have a window over your kitchen sink. You can watch the world go by. Put up a bird feeder. Plant a bulb, an herb, a perennial, a tree, and watch it grow. Hang up a prism and contemplate life. (It doesn't take a genius to wash dishes.)

Washing dishes is a chance to be alone with yourself, let your mind wander—or reel it in, whichever needs to be done. Washing the dishes is the Universe giving you a chance to wash up and re-group, to wet down and shake off like a dog, to rinse away your troubles and clean up your mind, to take a Brillo pad to the grimy nooks and crannies of your heart. To wash your troubles down the drain.

Once when I was shopping at a little roadside vegetable stand, I came across a plate with a verse written on it. It gave me a whole new take on washing the dishes. Something I'd never even thought of before.

> *Thank God for dirty dishes,*
> *For they have a tale to tell.*
> *While others may go hungry,*
> *We're still eating well.*
> *With health, home, and happiness,*
> *We surely shouldn't fuss.*
> *For by the stack of evidence,*
> *Life's been very good to us.*

Oxford Onion Soup

Yield: 4 to 6 servings

I have a friend who is a big, fancy professor at Duke University. When he was telling me about going to Oxford to be a guest lecturer, I said, "Oh, you'll just love Mississippi!"

"Not that Oxford," he said, horrified, "I mean the one in England." Oh well, too bad for him. He didn't get any of this onion soup, specialty of my Oxford, Mississippi, nephew.

6 slices vegetarian bacon
½ cup soy margarine plus 1 tablespoon
    toasted sesame oil
6 to 7 cups sliced mixed onions *(Make it a
    good mix of red, yellow, white, leeks,
    scallions, and shallots. Save the
    scallion greens to chop for garnish.)*
¾ cup flour
6 cups vegetable broth
1 cup soymilk
Salt and pepper, to taste

Sauté the vegetarian bacon in a little of the soy margarine in a large, heavy soup pot, and set aside to use later as garnish. In the same pan (without cleaning it out), add the remaining margarine and the sesame oil and onions. Let cook until most of the onions are at least half done. Dust with flour, stir, cook, and continue to keep your eye on it for about 10 or 15 minutes, or until the onions are done and the flour is golden. Add the broth, bring to a boil, and reduce the heat. Simmer for about 30 minutes.

About 15 minutes before serving, remove about 2 to 3 cups of the soup, and put in a blender or food processor with the soymilk. Blend and add back to the soup. Add salt and pepper to taste. When all the liquid is reheated through, the soup is done. Garnish with the crumbled vegetarian bacon and the chopped scallion greens.

Sally Heming's Peanut Soup

Yield: 6 to 8 servings

Sally Heming was Thomas Jefferson's mistress. I have to think she must have made great soup, so this is a tribute to her.

Sometimes I crave this and it hits the spot. It must be one of the ultimate comfort foods, so rich and thick—nothing at all fancy, but oh so satisfying. It's a great soup to have with a salad and/or baked squash on a cold night. Hot crusty bread tastes good with this too.

2 tablespoons soy margarine plus
    2 teaspoons toasted sesame oil*
1 onion, chopped
1 clove garlic, chopped
2 ribs celery, chopped
1 sweet potato, chopped
2 carrots, sliced
1 piece fresh ginger, about the size of your
    thumb, peeled and finely chopped
1 to 2 teaspoons chili paste, depending on
    how hot you like things
1½ teaspoons salt
4 cups vegetable broth
½ cup soymilk
3 cups V-8 juice
1 cup smooth peanut butter
3 slices vegetarian bacon, cooked and
    crumbled, or ½ cup chopped roasted
    peanuts, for garnish
Finely chopped scallions, for garnish

Heat the margarine and oil in a skillet. Add the onions, then the garlic. Don't be in a hurry; as you get the next ingredient chopped, add it and give it a stir, then move on to the next item until you have put in the celery, sweet potato, carrots, and ginger. Cover and allow to cook until the sweet potato and carrots are done. Put in a food processor, and blend until smooth. Put all this in a soup pot with the chili paste, salt, vegetable broth, soymilk, V-8 juice, and peanut butter. Turn the heat to low. Don't let it come to a boil, but make sure it is totally heated through. This should take about an hour. Serve hot with crumbled veggie bacon or roasted peanuts as a garnish. Finely chopped scallions are very good to use with the bacon.

There is a hot toasted sesame oil on the market if you want to use that instead of the chili paste.

Pot Likker & October Bean Soup

Yield: 6 to 8 servings

When Yankees and T. V. people go on and feel so sorry for "those pathetic people in Appalachia," I just don't get it. First of all, they're always mispronouncing Appalachia. You know it's a foreigner if they say Appa-LAY-chee-a. (The term foreigner is completely subjective, as where I grew up, foreigner meant someone from the next "hollow" over.) Now, anybody in their right mind knows it's Appa-LATCH-a.

It's the one part of the country that has not yet been homogenized/pasteurized/sanitized/Disney-fied, and malled over. It has personality. Forget South Beach—some of the nicest art-deco buildings I ever saw were in West, by God, Virginia. And style? Who else could wear overalls, a turn-of-the-century tail coat, carry a shot gun, and look more natural?

Here is a great soup that hits the spot on a cold day. If you like hot food, put in a few hot peppers with the onion and potatoes.

1 cup dry cranberry or October beans
2 yellow onions, chopped
5 red-skinned potatoes, chopped
1 large mess of greens, about 3 pounds
(Kale is best, washed and torn into small pieces. Let water remain on the leaves.)
4 to 5 cups vegetable broth
Salt and pepper, to taste
2 to 3 tablespoons olive oil
2 to 3 tablespoons soy margarine

Put the beans and one of the chopped onions in a soup pot, and cover with the broth. Let simmer for about 2 hours. In a separate pot or pan (whichever you have that will fit the potatoes and greens), put in the olive oil. When hot, add the rest of the chopped onion and the chopped potatoes. Allow to cook a few minutes, until the onions are at least half done, then salt generously. Top the potatoes with the freshly rinsed kale, then cover and turn down the heat. Let cook about 15 minutes, or until the kale is wilted or done to your liking.

Add the potato and kale mixture carefully to the beans. Give a good stir and cover. Let cook over very low heat until the potatoes are very soft. Stir in the soy margarine and serve.

Sarah's Old-Time Vegetable Soup

Yield: 8 to 10 large servings

Once my friend Dorita told me she made this soup with 12 cloves of garlic. I was incredulous until I tried it myself; it was great and definitely kept away the werewolves.

1 onion, thinly sliced
3 to 4 cloves garlic, smashed
¼ teaspoon toasted sesame oil
2 tablespoons olive oil
7 cups water
1 bay leaf
3 potatoes, diced
1 to 2 carrots, sliced in thin rounds
1 to 2 stalks celery, chopped
1 small bunch of your favorite greens
    (¼ to ½ head of cabbage works well)
¼ to ½ pound of your favorite noodles
One 8-ounce can tomato or vegetable juice
Salt and pepper, to taste *(This likes a lot of salt.)*

Sauté the onion and garlic in the sesame and olive oils until soft. Add the water and drop in the bay leaf. Put in the potatoes, carrots, celery, and greens, in that order. Let simmer 1 hour, or until the potatoes are done.

The secret of this soup is never to let it come to a rolling boil. Add the noodles, tomato juice, salt, and pepper, and continue to cook at no more than a simmer for 20 to 30 minutes. Serve with cornbread. If there are any leftovers, all the better; this soup is always better the next day.

Gumbo

Yield: 8 to 10 servings

You can't say you've been to the Deep South until you've tasted gumbo. It's another of those recipes that everybody has their own special way of making, unchanged for 10 or so generations. I bet blood has been drawn over when to add the filé.

I add tofu and tempeh instead of shrimp or sausage in this recipe. It's always a bit different every time I make it and always delicious!

½ to ¾ cup oil *(Make at least a couple tablespoons of this toasted sesame oil.)*
½ to ¾ cup flour
1 large onion, chopped
1 bunch green onions, chopped
1 green pepper, chopped
1 red pepper, chopped
5 to 6 ribs celery with leaves, chopped
2 teaspoons thyme
3 cloves garlic, mashed and chopped
1 to 2 pounds okra, sliced
6 to 7 cups liquid *(whatever kind you like)*
6 tomatoes, chopped
½ bunch parsley, finely chopped
2 bay leaves
2 tablespoons tamari or Pick-a-Peppa sauce, or a little of both
Several good shakes of hot sauce
1 teaspoon paprika
Salt, to taste
1 pound tofu, cut in small cubes
6 to 8 cups steaming hot cooked rice
Filé, to taste *(See next page.)*

Heat the oil over low heat in a big soup pot or Dutch oven. When it's hot, add the flour. This is supposed to cook over low heat for about 10 to 15 minutes until (this is the big secret) it's the color of a copper penny. Add the chopped onions, green onions, peppers, celery, thyme, and garlic. Cook this over low heat for about 30 to 45 minutes. It will be fairly dry; stir frequently. Try not to add any more oil, but if you have to, go ahead.

Sauté the okra in a little oil in a separate skillet. When it's done, add to the pot along with the liquid, tomatoes, parsley, bay leaves, tamari or pick-a-peppa, hot sauce, paprika, salt, and tofu. Let it come to a boil, then turn down and let simmer 2 to 3 hours. The key to this recipe is low heat and almost constant stirring the first 45 minutes or so. After that, stir when you think of it. After an hour or so, taste and add more salt or a pinch of cayenne.

Serve this with a big platter of hot rice, and pass the filé.

A note about filé

Filé is made out of ground sassafras leaves. It adds a flavor all its own, and if you can find it, please try it. If you add it directly to the pot, don't allow the soup to return to a boil, or even cook much longer, or the filé will make the gumbo stringy and not fit to eat. In many families, the filé is passed around the table and each person suits himself.

It was the Choctaw Indians who first made filé. They called it "kombo," which is where we got gumbo from.

Back Roads Lentil Soup

Yield: 5 servings

Vinegar can be added to the pot or put on the table for your guests to serve themselves. It brings out the taste of the lentils like nobody's business. Whoever gets the bay leaf gets a kiss or gets to wash the dishes. This all depends on the temperament of the cook.

3 to 4 tablespoons olive oil
1 onion, diced
1 carrot, chopped into matchsticks
3 cloves garlic, smashed
Tamari, to taste
1½ cups dry lentils
3 to 4 cups water
2 bay leaves
1 pound spinach or other green, such as
    kale or chard
Salt and pepper, to taste
1 tablespoon rice vinegar per person

Heat the oil in a soup pot, then add the onion, carrot, and garlic, and sauté until soft and turning brown. Add the tamari, lentils, and water. Give it a stir and throw in the bay leaves. Let it all come to a boil, then turn down to a simmer. When the lentils are getting soft, add the spinach leaves and cover so they will wilt. Stir while adding salt and pepper. Add more water if you want a thinner soup. When the spinach is wilted, the soup is done.

How to Make a Cream Soup without using any Cream

The easiest way to do this is to use soymilk; it substitutes for dairy milk perfectly in any recipe. Some supermarkets don't carry it, but most natural foods stores do. Try Oriental food stores too; lots of times they sell fresh soymilk. Here are some other ways to add creaminess to soups without using cream:

1. Mash the soup several times with a potato masher; this will thicken it up.

2. Put 1 to 2 cups of the soup in the blender until smooth, and stir back into the soup.

3. Put 1 to 2 cups of the soup in the blender with ½ pound of tofu, and blend until smooth. Stir back into the soup. This is the equivalent of stirring in sour cream.

4. Throw in a handful of rice. Usually, if the soup is nice and thick, you won't miss the milk.

5. Use nut milk. It's easy to make. Process ¼ to ½ cup of nuts (any kind tastes good—peanuts, almonds, cashews, sunflower seeds, etc.) in a blender with 1 to 2 cups of water until very smooth. This is a good replacement for dairy milk in almost any recipe. It's good, too, in breads or casseroles.

6. Make a batch of nutritional yeast "cheese," p. 71, or a white sauce, and stir that in.

7. Eat a nice clear soup, like miso, more often!

8. Strain some liquid from nonfat yogurt: Line a strainer with a paper towel. Scoop the yogurt in and let strain overnight in the fridge. This makes imitation sour cream and can be used in all kinds of recipes that call for yogurt, sour cream, or mayo.

9. Use soymilk or rice milk. These work great and are the easiest of all to use and substitute. Be sure to get soymilk that is plain, with no honey or vanilla or any flavoring added. Flavored, sweetened milk works good in desserts or breads for baking, but can ruin gravy or soup.

Boone's Creek Corn Chowder

Yield: 6 servings

When you serve this, put a half ear of corn in each person's bowl and a big plate of biscuits in the middle of the table. You can add a cup of soymilk or plain milk to this, if you want, and maybe a shake of good-tasting nutritional yeast.

2 to 3 tablespoons sesame or safflower oil
2 cloves garlic, smashed and chopped
1 onion, chopped
4 potatoes, cubed
1 carrot, sliced into matchsticks
1 to 2 handfuls rice
2 stalks celery with leaves, chopped
¼ teaspoon cayenne
Salt and pepper, to taste
4 to 5 ears corn, broken in half or thirds
1 to 2 tablespoons miso *(yellow or white)*

Heat the oil in a soup pot, and add the garlic and onion. When slightly cooked, add the potatoes and enough water to generously cover. When the potatoes are at least half done, add the carrot, rice, celery, cayenne, salt, and pepper. Cut the kernels off 3 of the ears of corn directly over the pot. Take the other 2 ears and break into 2 or 3 pieces; add to the soup like that. Simmer about 1 to 1½ hours. Dissolve the miso into a cup of the broth, and add to the soup, stirring well to combine. Serve hot.

Potato Soup

Yield: 5 servings

Potato soup is the king of comfort foods. It's so cheap and so easy, . . . is that why it tastes so good? Here's how I do it:

6 to 8 red-skinned potatoes, unpeeled
    and cubed
½ cup soy margarine
4 to 6 cups warm milk or soymilk
Salt and pepper, to taste
½ cup chopped fresh parsley
1 teaspoon dill weed or caraway seeds
    (optional)
Chopped green onion, for garnish

Cook the potatoes. (These can be left-overs or cooked in advance.) Pour off most of the water, then mash, adding the soy margarine and about ½ of the warm milk. Don't feel you have to get all the lumps out. Add the rest of the milk, and simmer over low heat until heated through. Be careful not to overcook! Add the parsley along with the dill weed or caraway seeds, if using. Garnish with chopped green onion. Serve this soup at once, and plan to eat it all. It looses something by the next day.

Frogmore Stew

Yield: 6 to 8 servings

What is it? Like all delicious food, it was born from hunger and whatever you happen to have on hand. Low country boil or down-home stew— whatever you call it, it's always good. Origin? Some say it's from a little fishing town on St. Helena Island, off Hilton Head. My friend, who is from Frogmore, Louisiana, protests that it couldn't be from anywhere other than her beloved Frogmore. No matter the origin or the preparation method, it is always good.

This is traditionally a fish stew with shrimp and/or crab, but I just leave that out and try to put in a vegetarian meat or fish substitute that's tasty.

8 cups water
1 dozen red-skinned potatoes
Several whole cloves garlic
2 umeboshi plums *(to substitute for fatback)*
2 heaping tablespoons Old Bay Seasoning
Salt and pepper, to taste
6 to 8 ears corn
½ pound tempeh
Oil for frying
8 ounces vegetarian sausage
1 loaf French bread, pulled apart in big chunks
Chopped green onion, for garnish

Combine the water, potatoes, garlic, umeboshi plums, Old Bay Seasoning, salt, and pepper in large pot. Let simmer about 20 minutes, until the potatoes are tender. Cut the kernels off 2 to 3 ears of the corn, and add to the soup pot. Don't forget to milk the corn. (See Granny's Creamed Corn, p. 54, for how to do this.) Then break the remaining ears in half, and add to the soup. Continue cooking over low heat. Dip out some of the water if it seems like there is too much. The potatoes and corn should not be floating in water.

While the potatoes and corn are cooking, slice the tempeh into skinny fingers. Fry in oil until crispy, and drizzle with tamari if you like. Remove from the skillet and fry the sausage. You can do these together if your skillet is big enough.

For each serving, place a big hunk of bread in a large soup bowl, and dip the stew over the bread with a slotted spoon. A little stew broth is good, but not too much, unless that's how you like it. Take several sausages and tempeh pieces, and arrange over the potatoes and corn. Sprinkle chopped green onions over the whole thing.

Croutons

Yield: 3 cups

These smell so good while they're baking that everyone in the house will come in the kitchen to ask, "What are you making?" This will yield a big batch, but it keeps well and makes great munchies.

2 tablespoons soy margarine
1 clove garlic, smashed and chopped, or
    ½ teaspoon garlic powder
1 tablespoon chives, chopped
1 tablespoon poppy seeds
1 teaspoon kelp powder
1 teaspoon sage
1 teaspoon thyme
1 teaspoon salt
2 teaspoons oregano
5 to 6 slices slightly stale bread

Melt the margarine in a small saucepan. Add the garlic, herbs, and spices, sauté for a few minutes, and remove from the heat.

Preheat the oven to 350°F. Lay the bread slices out on a table or counter. Spoon a little of the herb-margarine mixture onto each piece, and spread around with the back of the spoon. Stack all the slices on top of one another with the top one margarine side down and the bottom one margarine side up. Slice the whole pile into cubes. Spread the cubes on a cookie sheet, and bake for 20 minutes or until toasted, tossing them once or twice to get them evenly browned.

Put the croutons in a big bowl, and serve. If you like cheese, sprinkle on some grated Parmesan while the croutons are hot, and toss lightly. The heat will make the cheese stick. Good-tasting nutritional yeast is also good on these, if you like.

Dumplings

Yield: 3 to 4 servings

Dumplings are kind of forgotten on today's vegetarian menus—what a shame. Even the name says comfort food. These dumplings are made with thick soups (split pea, vegetable, lentil, or noodle). They are easy. Dumplings can also be cooked on top of pieces of simmering tofu in a skillet. Just make sure the lid fits tightly and the tofu is juicy.

1 cup flour *(Whole wheat is fine.)*
¼ cup wheat germ *(optional)*
3 teaspoons baking powder
½ teaspoon salt
1 tablespoon honey
Egg replacer equal to 2 eggs
½ cup cold water
¼ to ½ cup chopped parsley, chopped onion, nutritional yeast, or grated cheese

Mix the dry ingredients in a bowl, make a well in the middle, and add the wet ingredients. Just barely stir until the dough leaves the sides of the bowl. Place a spoonful of dough onto the soup. Be sure the soup is steaming hot when you do this—not necessarily rapidly boiling, but hot enough to start cooking the dumplings right away. Continue spooning the dough over the top of the soup until the soup is covered. Put on the lid, making sure the fits tightly. You can also invert a glass pie plate over the pot, and watch them cook if you want. Remember to leave the lid on. No Peeking!

These dumplings won't get tough, because they don't have eggs in them. Check them after about 10 to 12 minutes. You can prick them with a fork to make sure they're done in the middle.

Here are a few foolproof tips to give you that good old dumpling confidence.

1. To prevent heavy dumplings with soggy bottoms, make sure the cooking liquid simmers gently and constantly.

2. Don't lift the lid to peek while cooking. The dumplings are steaming. If you let the steam out, they can't cook.

Tomato Dumplings

Yield: 3 to 4 servings

This is another way to use fresh tomatoes in the summertime. Don't let what looks to be a long list of ingredients put you off; it's easy and delicious.

¼ cup soy margarine
½ cup chopped onion
½ green pepper, chopped
1 celery stalk, chopped
5 to 6 fresh tomatoes, coarsely chopped
    with their juice, or one 28-ounce can
    whole tomatoes, undrained and
    chopped
2 teaspoons brown sugar
½ teaspoon salt
Pinch of black pepper

1 cup flour
1½ teaspoons baking powder
½ teaspoon salt
1 tablespoon soy margarine
Egg replacer equal to 1 egg
⅓ cup soymilk

Melt the ¼ cup margarine in a skillet that has a tight-fitting lid. Add the onion, pepper, and celery, and let cook until the onions and peppers are tender. Stir in the tomatoes, brown sugar, salt, and pepper. Let come to a boil, and simmer about 3 to 5 minutes.

Combine the flour, baking powder, and salt in a medium bowl. Cut in the 1 tablespoon margarine until crumbly. Add the egg replacer and milk, and stir until moistened. Drop by spoonfuls into the simmering tomato mixture. Cover and cook over medium-low heat for about 20 minutes.

Tofu Dumplings

Yield: 3 to 4 servings

This is a good recipe for people who are looking for new ways to use tofu. It's easy and delicious.

½ pound tofu
Egg replacer equal to 1 egg
2 teaspoons baking powder
¼ teaspoon salt
½ cup whole wheat flour
2 tablespoons chopped basil, thyme,
    oregano, or parsley *(optional)*

Process the tofu, egg replacer, baking powder, and salt in a food processor or blender until smooth. Scrape down the sides of the processing bowl if necessary. Add the flour and herbs, if using, and blend again.

Drop by spoonfuls onto the top of a soup or stew, cover tightly, and simmer for about 15 to 20 minutes. Remember, don't peek while these are cooking.

113

Bacon and Egg Candy and Trailer Trash Food

Every time I even think about bacon and egg candy (page 116), I burst out laughing. Who thinks these things up? I wanted to use it real bad in this book, but it didn't seem to fit in anywhere. That's when I got the idea for the Trailer Park Specials chapter.

They're the second class citizens of the cooking world, but delicious none the same: recipes that must have one can cream of mushroom soup, one can cream of celery soup, and one can of tomato soup, no matter what it is. Most of the ingredients are either canned, frozen, wrapped in at least three different layers of plastic, or must be whopped on the counter to be opened. They're the processed, the instant, the refined—precooked, pre-stirred, prebaked, and prefabbed. They contain ingredients that beg a second look. They're the dishes that disappear first at a pot luck; they are our secret obsessions. Gooey, sweet, hot, greasy, and salty all at the same time, no self-respecting vegetarian would eat them more than once or twice in a lifetime. These recipes will never have balsamic vinegar or ginger oil as an ingredient. Each and every one invokes Elvis. They are as much a part of the South as the magnolia tree and the silver service. They are on the wrong side of the tracks, at the outskirts of every town. They are the beer-belly peeping out from under the too small T-shirt and cut-offs. They are Trailer Trash and Proud of It.!!

Trailer Park Specials

What do divorce proceedings and a hurricane have in common? Whichever one occurs, the trailer is coming down.

popular Southern joke

Cuisine is when things taste like themselves.

Curnousky

Bacon and Egg Candy

Yield: about 2½ dozen

1 pound white chocolate
One 10-ounce bag thin stick pretzels
Yellow M & M's *(Buy a couple of bags, and
    pick out the yellow ones.)*
Wax paper

Melt the white chocolate in a double boiler. Place groups of 2 pretzel sticks side by side on a cookie sheet covered with wax paper. Use a teaspoon to put a small amount of melted white chocolate in the middle of the pretzel pairs. Lightly press one yellow M & M into the middle of the chocolate and 2 pretzels. Looks just like bacon and eggs!

Billy Bob's Hors d'Oeurves

Yield: 8 to 10 servings

No Superbowl, Final Four, or ACC championship party in the South would be complete without this appetizer.

One 8-ounce package soy or regular
    cream cheese
1 bottle Pick-a-Peppa sauce

Unwrap the cream cheese and plop onto a saucer or plate. Pour the Pick-a-Peppa sauce over the cream cheese until the top is covered and it is dripping over the sides. You're all done! Serve with chips or sliced vegetables.

Big Bubba Tofu

Yield: 4 servings

Ready for a nice light dinner? Then skip to the next recipe. This hearty dish will fill your stomach and stay there all night. It hits the spot, it's easy, and men love it. You can't beat this on a cold night.

Egg replacer powder equal to 2 eggs *(Do not reconstitute.)*

½ cup soymilk

1 pound tofu, frozen, thawed, and squeezed dry

¼ teaspoon each salt and pepper

¾ cup Bisquick, or ¼ cup each cornmeal, flour, and good-tasting nutritional yeast

Oil for frying

1 tablespoon tamari *(optional)*

Gravy:

¼ cup soy margarine

2 large onions, sliced

2 cups soymilk

Mix the dry egg replacer into the ½ cup soymilk. Slice the tofu and dip it into the milk mixture. Mix the salt, pepper, and dry ingredients in a bowl, and use to dredge the tofu slices. Fry the slices in a hot skillet until brown and crispy on both sides. Drizzle with tamari while cooking if you want.

Remove the tofu from the pan. Add about ¼ cup more oil and the sliced onions. When transparent, add any leftover coating mixture. (This should be about ½ cup.) Stir around a few minutes until the flour is browned. Add the soymilk and stir slowly until barely thickened. Add the tofu back to the pan, and let simmer with the gravy about 10 minutes. Serve over toast or with potatoes.

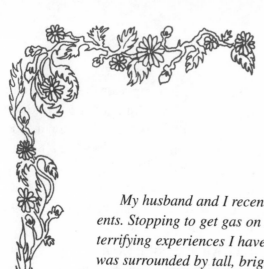

Fillin' Stations

My husband and I recently went to New York to visit his parents. Stopping to get gas on Interstate 95 was one of the more terrifying experiences I have had in a while. The gas station itself was surrounded by tall, bright lights, and the whole place was enclosed by a chainlink fence topped with barbed wire ("bob war" to us Southerners). Inside there was a whole mess of cars, driven by people with the most miserable looks on their faces. And a list of rules to be followed, for goodness sake, was posted outside by the pumps:

1. Don't Get Out of Your Car

2. Don't Talk to the Attendant

3. Don't Put Your Hands in Your Pockets until Ready to Pay.

4. No Self Service

5. No Cash After Dark

6. No Smoking

As I innocently leaned over to say "Hey" to the beleaguered attendant when it was finally our turn to gas up, my husband stopped me, horrified. "You don't do that up here; people will think you are going to rob them."

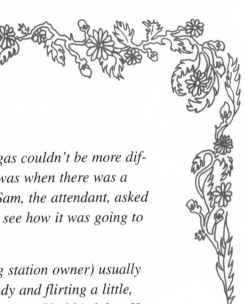

At home in North Carolina, getting gas couldn't be more different. The only time I ever had to wait was when there was a "real good Beverly Hillbillies on" and Sam, the attendant, asked me if I minded waiting as she wanted to see how it was going to come out.

Donald Davis (Sam's dad and filling station owner) usually pumps the gas, giving me a piece of candy and flirting a little, which is fine with me as he just celebrated his 73rd birthday. He always has a big smile and something to say that keeps me grinning until my next fill-up. I still laugh about when he said, "Made love to my wife last night, hardest work I done all week!"

Now, I don't mean to be unfair or smart-alecky. I know there are lots of mom and pop country store-filling stations above the Mason-Dixon line, but something about this just struck me as such a basic difference that it has stayed with me. It is just this kind of thing that makes living in the South special.

It's that little group of old timers around the wood stove discussing weather and spitting tobacco. The way dried blood, mouse traps, and Hershey Bars are all displayed together just as natural as the live bait in the refrigerator along with the butter. That's the enchantment of every-day filling stations.

Tater-Tot Biscuits

Yield: 8 to 10 servings

This recipe is from my friend Michelle, who says it was discovered after one too many late night parties involving beverages and the munchies. This is exactly how to do it.

Cook up a batch of tater-tots. (Cook them until the outside of them is really crunchy—about 10 minutes longer than it says to cook them on the bag.) Be sure to make more than you want to eat right then, and save the extra out until the next morning. When you're still bleary-eyed the next morning, just make these. You can also add crushed red pepper or fresh basil when you add the tater-tots to the dry mixture.

2 cups flour
1½ teaspoons baking powder
1 teaspoon salt
½ teaspoon baking soda
4 tablespoons soy margarine
¾ cup soymilk
1½ to 2 cups overcooked tater tots

Preheat the oven to 400°F. Mix the dry ingredients together, then add the margarine. Rub this together with your fingers or cut it in with a pastry blender or whisk until crumbly and the size of peas. Crumble the leftover tater-tots into this mixture. Add the soymilk and barely mix.

Roll the dough about ¾ inch thick on a lightly floured surface. Use a floured glass rim to cut the biscuits, or, if you are feeling creative, use a star-shaped cookie cutter (my favorite). Place the biscuits on a lightly greased baking sheet. Bake for 15 minutes or so. Keep your sleepy eye on them so they won't burn.

Smoky Mountain Salted Nuts

Yield: about 5 cups

Here is a good, easy recipe. Nothing on earth tastes as good or smells as good while cooking as roasted pecans. If you are wondering about nice homemade Christmas gifts, these pecans are perfect. Put them in an antique tin box, and you may be mistaken for Martha Stewart.

1 cup soy margarine
1 tablespoon salt
1 pound pecans
Choose one *(optional)*:
>   1½ teaspoons cumin
>   ¼ teaspoon cayenne pepper
>   2 tablespoons sugar

Preheat the oven to 200°F. Melt the margarine in a large skillet. Add the salt, pecans, and one of the optional flavorings, and stir well, then remove from the heat. Put the pecans in a rectangular baking dish, and bake for 1 hour. Be sure to stir every 15 minutes. When your house smells good enough to eat, the pecans are done. Remove from the oven and drain on paper towels. You can freeze these or store them in a tin box.

Cousin Susan's Cheeze Straws

Yield: about 30 cheeze straws

No true Southern event, from bridge club to bridal shower, would be complete without cheese straws. Add ½ cup chopped pecans to be fancy. These are the best and can be frozen if you need to make them ahead of time.

½ pound grated sharp cheddar cheese
>   *(Nondairy is OK.)*
1 cup soy margarine
2 cups flour
1 teaspoon salt
Big dash red pepper *(Be generous if you like it hot, ¼ teaspoon or so.)*
2 cups Rice Crispies

Preheat the oven to 350°F. Mix the cheese and margarine well. Add the flour, salt, and red pepper slowly until well mixed. Add the Rice Crispies last. Make into small balls, and press with a fork onto a cookie sheet. Bake for 20 minutes.

Company's Comin' Cheeze Puffs

Yield: anywhere from 10 to 30!

These are rich, short, delicious, and were very chic in 1956. If you are making this for a lot of people, double the recipe. The recipe I converted it from said "makes 30"—mine made 10. (We made them as an appetizer. They were so rich we couldn't eat anything for dinner.) So you will have to experiment as to how many this really does make, as the dough always wraps around the olive differently.

1 cup grated nondairy cheddar cheese
¼ cup soy margarine, softened
½ cup flour
1 teaspoon paprika
1 pinch cayenne
½ teaspoon salt
One 4½-ounce jar small stuffed green
    olives or your favorite pitted olives

Preheat the oven to 400°F. Blend the cheese with the softened margarine. Sift the dry ingredients together, add to the cheese mixture, and mix well. Wrap about 1 teaspoon or so of the mixture around each olive, covering it completely. (I usually end up using almost 2 tablespoons because my olives are so big!) Arrange on a cookie sheet, and chill until firm or freeze to bake later. Bake for 15 minutes. Serve hot or cold.

122

Good Ole' Boy Red Rice

Yield: 3 servings

Couldn't be easier and couldn't taste better. This is a good rice to have with Mexican food.

1 cup vegetable stock or water
¾ cup V-8 juice
1 cup basmati rice
One 8-ounce can peas and carrots
½ teaspoon salt
⅓ cup your favorite hot sauce

Put the liquids in a large stock pot, and heat. When simmering, add the rice, vegetables, salt, and hot sauce. Let it return to a boil, then cover and turn down the heat to very low. Let cook for 30 minutes or until the liquid has been absorbed by the rice. Do not lift the lid, or the good ole' red rice will turn into bad ole' red rice.

Heinz Tofu

Yield: 3 to 4 servings

My husband says, "This tastes just like ketchup, I don't know why you like it so much." He doesn't understand that is why this tastes so good.

1 yellow onion, chopped
1 pound tofu, cubed
3 tablespoons tamari
Oil, as needed
⅓ cup ketchup
1 tablespoon Dijon mustard
1 tablespoon toasted sesame oil

Fry the onions, tofu, and tamari in an electric skillet until the onions are tender and the tofu is browned on all sides. Turn occasionally with a spatula. Put the ketchup, mustard, and sesame oil in a measuring cup, and add enough water to make ¾ cup. Stir well and add to the skillet. Partially cover and continue to cook until the liquid is absorbed. Continue to turn occasionally with a spatula.

Big Stone Gap Sausage Balls

Yield: appetizers for 15 to 20

This is a good recipe to make with kids, as it's a hands-on recipe. If you've never had the real version, you haven't missed anything, because this vegetarian version is just as good.

1 pound your favorite vegetarian sausage, uncooked
1 pound nondairy cheddar cheese
2 cups Bisquick, or 2 cups flour, 2 teaspoons baking powder, and ½ teaspoon salt

Preheat the oven to 350°F. Cut the sausage into small pieces, and combine with the cheddar and Bisquick in a mixing bowl. Mix and squish well by hand. Roll into ½-inch balls, and place on an ungreased cookie sheet. Bake for 12 to 15 minutes or until golden brown. You can freeze these and reheat later.

Back Porch
Bar-B-Que Beans

Yield: 6 to 8 servings

This is a fabulous recipe, if you can call it a recipe. Everyone I have ever made this for has gone insane and begged me for the recipe. I laugh and give it to them. The best thing about it is that black-eyed peas cook so fast, the whole thing is done much quicker than if you used regular white beans. If you have people over and need something fast and yummy, this is a good dish. Your cornbread can bake while the beans are cooking.

3 cups black-eyed peas
⅓ to ½ bottle of your favorite bar-b-que
    sauce *(I like K.C's Masterpiece.)*
6 cups water
Dash of salt and pepper

Rinse the black-eyed peas, and put in a pot with enough water to cover. Let cook until soft, about 45 minutes. Add the bar-b-que sauce, and allow to simmer about 30 to 45 more minutes. The time is not really important. We heat with a wood stove and I'm the fire captain, so many times I cook things just to help heat up the house. On a cold day, I'd let these cook a lot longer, but if you are pressed for time, they won't need to cook much longer than 15 minutes, just enough to let the flavors blend well. Add salt and pepper, and enjoy with cornbread and greens.

Tofu Chicken-Fried Steak

Yield: 4 servings

Let the tofu get good and frozen at least a few days before you use it here. Let it thaw in the refrigerator overnight or for a whole day. This is good with anything from biscuits to butter beans.

1 pound frozen tofu, thawed, squeezed dry
2 to 3 tablespoons toasted sesame oil
1 tablespoon hot sesame oil
¼ cup tamari
1 tablespoon Dijon mustard
3 tablespoons flour
3 tablespoons sesame seeds
3 tablespoons bread crumbs
3 tablespoons nutritional yeast flakes
Oil for frying

Really press the water out of the tofu. Slice and re-press the slices if you think you need to. Lay the slices in a glass baking dish or bowl, not metal. Put about ⅓ cup water in a measuring cup, and add both sesame oils, tamari, and mustard. Mix well so the oils will combine with the water. Pour over the tofu. You can make up another batch of this if you want more marinade. When you're ready to fry the slices, mix the flour, sesame seeds, bread crumbs, and yeast on a plate. Dredge the slices through this (twice if necessary to get a good, thick coating), and place gently in hot oil, preferably in an electric skillet. Let get good and brown on both sides.

Crush and Run Mock Pecan Pie

Yield: 8 to 10 servings

When we first moved to the country, I was the one that was always having to deal with workmen or delivery men or phone men or farmer neighbors or someone like that. This one guy who was delivering gravel for the driveway just kept going on and on to me about "crush and run," "crush and run." I had no idea what he was talking about. I thought it sounded like a country song. It was about two years later when I found out it was some special gravel, but I had already written this little ditty for the gravel man who gave me the inspiration.

Egg replacer equal to 3 eggs *(Try the flaxseed version on p. 11.)*

1 cup sugar

24 Ritz crackers, completely crushed until very fine (U*se a food processor, rolling pin, or tire wheels—whatever works for you.)*

2 cups pecans

1 teaspoon vanilla

Preheat the oven to 350°F. Mix the egg replacer with the sugar. In another bowl, mix the cracker crumbs, pecans, and vanilla, then combine both mixtures together well. Bake in a 9 x 13-inch baking dish or 2 small pie plates for 25 to 30 minutes. Top with soy ice cream!

Crush and Run

Going down to get my hair done
To the good old Curl up and Dye.
I was almost there, when I stopped to stare,
Why, oh why, oh it's just not fair
What I saw was like a thorn in my eye.

You was kissing her and holding on
Like she was the very last straw
What you two was doing in the back of that car,
Well, there ought to be a law.

Call up the rock and gravel pit,
Go ahead an' get it done.
You treat my heart like a parking lot
Crush and Run.

I'll stay around for another day,
I got nowhere's else to go
I guess I could always get us a spot
On the Jerry Springer Show

I feel like my life is a country song,
Nothing but hurtin' and blues
I couldn't get worse, my heart's in a hearse
I guess I'm just paying my dues.

Call up the rock and gravel pit
Go ahead an' get it done
You treat my heart like a parking lot
Crush and Run.

Smoky Mountain Pie or Dump Cobbler

Yield: 6 to 8 servings

You certainly can't say this recipe is too complicated or the ingredients are too hard to find. I always imagine this being the specialty of a worn out hillbilly woman. She was just too exhausted to do anything more than open a can of peaches and dump them in a baking dish. If you have trouble making good cobblers and fruit pie-type things, this recipe really is easy and good, and it doesn't necessarily mean you are a worn out hillbilly woman if you make it.

½ cup soy margarine
1 cup flour
1 cup sugar
1½ teaspoons baking powder
¾ cup soymilk
One 15-ounce can fruit, or 2 cups fresh fruit

Preheat the oven to 350°F. Melt the margarine in a 9 x 13-inch baking dish. Mix the flour, sugar, and baking powder, then stir in the milk and add to the dish. Pour in a can of peaches or other fruit in the center of the dish. Don't stir. Bake for 1 hour or until brown. This is really good with vanilla soy ice cream.

Double-Wide Banana Pudding

Yield: 10 servings

I was afraid to try and figure out a way to make pudding with no milk or eggs, but this recipe hits the spot. Most traditional recipes call for 1 cup of sugar, but that was way too sweet, even for me. The amount here works fine.

¾ cup sugar
¼ cup cornstarch
¼ teaspoon salt
3 cups soymilk
2 teaspoons vanilla
⅓ cup soy margarine
One 12-ounce box vanilla wafers
4 to 6 bananas, sliced into small rounds

Combine the sugar, cornstarch and salt in a saucepan. Slowly add the milk, using a whip if necessary. Cover and let come to a boil over low heat for about 5 minutes. Remove from the heat and stir in the vanilla and margarine. In a 9 x 13-inch dish, put in a small amount of the pudding mixture. Then layer alternately with vanilla wafers and sliced bananas. Top with pudding and decorate with more sliced bananas, toasted slivered almonds, or some crumbled vanilla wafers, if desired. Chill overnight or at least 6 hours. Enjoy with soy whipped cream or Cool Whip.

Knock You Nakeds

Yield: about 2 dozen

The next time you are wondering what to make for the neighborhood bake sale, wonder no more—this is the ticket. Make copies of the recipe, as everyone who tries these cookies will beg you for it.

1 box German chocolate cake mix
1 cup chopped pecans
⅓ cup plus ½ cup evaporated milk or
    soymilk, divided
¾ cup melted soy margarine
One 14-ounce package caramels
1 cup semi-sweet chocolate chips

Preheat the oven to 350°F. Combine the dry cake mix, pecans, ⅓ cup of the milk, and the melted margarine in a large mixing bowl. Press half of the batter into the bottom of a greased 9 x 13-inch or 8 x 8-inch glass baking dish, and bake for 8 to 10 minutes. Leave the oven on.

Melt the caramels in the top of a double boiler with the remaining ½ cup milk. (Improvise a double boiler, if you don't have one, by setting a small metal bowl in a larger saucepan with several inches of water in it.) When the caramels are well mixed, pour them over the baked layer, and cover with the chocolate chips. Pour the remaining batter over the top of the chocolate chips, return to the oven, and bake for 18 minutes. Let cool before cutting into squares.

Spider Cookies

Yield: about 2 dozen

This is another recipe that kids can help with. Use the raisins for eyes!

One 6-ounce package butterscotch morsels
¼ cup creamy peanut butter
One 8-ounce can chow mein noodles
Raisins *(optional)*

Melt the butterscotch morsels and peanut butter in a double boiler. Don't stir too much. When melted, add the chow mein noodles, stirring to coat. Drop rounded teaspoonfuls onto waxed paper, and garnish with raisins, if you want. Store at room temperature or chill in the refrigerator.

Moonshiner's Tipsy Cake

Yield: 8 servings

This not only has odd ingredients, but odd instructions as well. I always imagine a moonshiner, a little tipsy from sampling his wares, was the first to make this cake. Can't you see him accidentally poking the batter with the end of a spoon and dropping the measuring spoon full of vanilla right into the batter? Then remembering the liquid at the last minute, and just pouring in the water? Well, surprises do happen. This is another good recipe to make with children.

1½ cups sifted flour
1 cup sugar
3 tablespoons cocoa
1 teaspoon soda
½ teaspoon salt
5 tablespoons oil *(corn or safflower always work good for baking)*
1 tablespoon vinegar
1 teaspoon vanilla
1 cup cold water

Preheat the oven to 350°F. Sift the flour and other dry ingredients into a greased 8 x 8-inch baking dish. Make 3 holes in the top of this mixture. Into one pour the oil, into one pour the vinegar, and into one pour the vanilla. Pour the cold water over the whole thing. Don't throw it away yet! Beat with a spoon until almost smooth, and the flour is mixed up. Bake for 30 minutes. Frost at will.

Moonshiners tip: Don't try to make moonshine on a bright, sunny day; the revenuers will see your smoke for sure. Wait for a misty, foggy morning, and you'll have plenty of time to get your mash good and hot.

Graceland French Toast

Yield: 4 to 6 servings

If anything could bring Elvis back from the dead, this recipe would do it.

1 pint rum raisin ice cream *(either dairy-, soy-, or rice-based is fine)*
5 to 6 pieces plain or cinnamon raisin bread

Scoop the ice cream in a bowl, and let it melt. Take one piece of bread at a time, dip it in the melted ice cream, and fry in a skillet with soy margarine until golden brown.

Hillbilly Best Bread

Yield: 8 servings

This recipe is what trailer park cooking is all about. I hardly ever make this because I hate to use ingredients that I consider processed, like canned biscuit dough. But occasionally, if we have house guests, I make this and it's a winner. People come from all over the house and yard to see what's cooking. It gets people out of bed quicker than the smell of coffee perking. The fun way to eat it is to just put it into the middle of the table and let people pull off little pieces of cinnamon bun, each at his or her own pace, a lot or a little. This way you can just put the cinnamon bread out with coffee, juice, and napkins and be ready to take your bows. Just make sure the biscuit dough cans are in the bottom of the trash can.

¼ cup melted soy margarine
½ cup chopped pecans

½ cup sugar
3 tablespoons cinnamon
Three 17-ounce cans or four 12-ounce cans
    flaky biscuits
Chopped nuts *(optional)*

½ cup soy margarine, melted
⅓ to ½ cup sugar
3 tablespoons cinnamon

Preheat the oven to 350°F. Mix the ¼ cup melted margarine with the pecans, and put in the bottom of a greased Bundt pan. Be sure to grease your pan real good so this will come out right. If you don't have a Bundt pan, you can use a 9 x 13-inch pan (but it's not as fun to eat that way).

Mix the ½ cup sugar and cinnamon in a bowl. Whack the biscuits out of the packages, and cut each biscuit into 4 to 6 pieces. As you cut each piece, toss it in the sugar-cinnamon mixture, then drop it in the bundt pan. If you have any extra chopped nuts around, sprinkle some in every so often along with the dough balls.

Combine the melted margarine, ⅓ to ½ cup sugar, and remaining 5 tablespoons cinnamon, and pour over the dough bits. Bake for 35 minutes. Remove and invert on a pretty platter to serve.

"Killer" Chocolate Cake

Yield: 15 servings

Yes, it really might kill you!

1 cup coconut
1 cup chopped pecans
1 box German chocolate cake mix
½ cup soy margarine
One 8-ounce package dairy or nondairy
  cream cheese
One 1-pound box confectioners' powdered
  sugar

Preheat the oven to 350°F. Oil and flour a 9 x 13-inch baking pan. Sprinkle the coconut and pecans over the bottom of the pan.

Prepare the cake mix according to the package directions, and pour over the nuts and coconut in the baking pan.

Melt the margarine and cream cheese, and add in the powdered sugar. Pour this over the cake mix, and bake for 45 minutes or until a toothpick or straw inserted in the middle comes out clean.

Sweet Iced Tea

1 family-size tea bag *(I use Lipton or
  Luzianne.)*
A sturdy pitcher—*(I use a 1-quart
  measuring cup.)*
¼ to ½ cup sugar, depending on how
  sweet you like it
4 cups boiling water
1 to 2 lemons, if you have them

Put the tea bag in the pitcher or measuring cup. Add sugar to your liking. Pour over the boiling water, and stir with a spoon to dissolve the sugar. Let sit about 2 to 3 hours. Remove the tea bag and add the lemon juice. This is your concentrate.

Fill a large glass with ice and about ½ to ¾ cup cold water. Fill the rest of the glass up with tea concentrate. I usually stop when the color looks like the way tea should look. Store the concentrate in the refrigerator overnight; it will last about 2 days. If your tea gets cloudy, pour a little boiling water in.

If you are making this for a group of people, use a pitcher instead of a glass at the end. Don't pour hot tea directly over ice cubes; they'll all melt.

To be very Southern, after you have made your tea, go out in the backyard and find a little peppermint patch. Pinch off a nice size sprig, and stick that in your glass of iced tea. Pure refreshment!

Sweet Iced Tea

There is nothing more Southern than sweet iced tea and probably nothing more misunderstood. I've come to the conclusion that if you were not born and raised in the South, then you just don't get it. Once in Boston on a sweltering hot day, I asked for tea, not realizing I should be more specific. What did I get? I big cup of hot tea.

Why would anyone make a pitcher of tea and not sweeten it? At restaurants, especially in the South, if I ask for sweet tea and am told, "Well, we don't have no sweet tea. You could put in the sugar yourself," I become irate. Have these people ever tried to dissolve sugar in an ice cold drink? Once I had to use 14 packets of sugar to make it sweet enough.

This is my favorite iced tea story. My friend Mike, who is quite a bit younger than me and has traveled a little but never out of the South, went on a trip with friends to New York. Now in the South when you want more iced tea, you get as much as you want for free; the restaurant usually gives you a whole pitcher so they don't have to keep coming to the table for a tea refill. Assuming this was the iced tea rule all over the world, every time the waitress came around and asked if they wanted more tea, everyone said yes. When they got their bill, they had racked up $28 worth of iced tea, $1.50 for every refill. They pleaded ignorance to the manager, and I believe he split the iced tea bill with them, but still, $14 for iced tea is a bit more than any Southerner could stand for.

A sweet tea recipe is not easy to write as nothing is ever measured or exact. It's the kind of recipe you have to eyeball out, but I think you'll be able to follow the previous recipe. Viola, who has worked for my grandmother since 1938, helped me with it as she makes the best iced tea on earth.

Box Lunches

I don't think this next chapter would be complete without a tribute to grandmothers everywhere and especially my grandmothers, who both happen to be masters of the packed lunch. Whether you were just taking a bagged lunch to school or something to eat half way to Myrtle Beach on the family vacation (we always ate at the Sweat Bee Haven), these lunches rate as the best ever. God, what memories. I can see that box now, all tied up and so heavy. Could all this be food?

There was fried chicken (I loved it then), cheese sandwiches, the kind with grated onion and mayo, and deviled eggs screwed back together and wrapped in wax paper with twisted ends. Carrot curls made with a vegetable peeler packed in baggies with ice cubes.

Sarah always used those little papers you use to line muffin tins to hold wonderful little surprises: chocolate almonds, raisins, toasted salted nuts. In those lunches, nothing was ever soggy. She also added the unexpected: note paper, pencils, emory boards, paper clips, and maps. Yes, all this in a lunch. There were always lots of napkins, silverware, and handiwipes. The brownies were in a small box all wrapped up inside the big one.

Granny made a big batch of praline cookies. These were kept in a separate cookie tin and were therefore lots easier to snitch.

If all this is making you hungry, why don't you pack a big lunch and zoom off on a big adventure right now.

Cookouts

Chestnuts in their spiky cases, squashy medlars, and
tart-tasting sorb apples—the autumn drives before it
a profusion of modest fruits which one does not pick,
but which fall into one's hands, which wait patiently
at the foot of the tree until man deigns to collect them.

Colette

O suns and skies and clouds of June,
Gang all your boasts together,
Ye cannot rival for one hour,
October's bright blue weather.

Helen Hunt Jackson

Even if something is left undone, everyone must take
time to sit still and watch the leaves turn.

Elizabeth Lawrence

Barbecue "Chicken" Tempeh

Yield: 3 servings

Two to three 8-ounce packages tempeh, steamed for 20 minutes or thawed and slightly sautéed
5 cups Wild Woman's Bar-Be-Que Sauce, p. 72
1 onion, chopped
A few tablespoons oil

The tempeh pieces should be cut into quarters, big enough so that they can't fall through the grill rack (or use a grill basket). Cut some in half width-wise, if you don't like them too thick.

When the coals in your grill are ready (you don't want them too hot), coat the tempeh generously on both sides with sauce, and lay gently over the rack. Brush on more sauce as the tempeh grills.

You can also make 6-inch square pouches with aluminum foil, and put a little barbecue sauce in the bottom of each bag to keep the tempeh from sticking. Slice the tempeh and coat each piece generously with sauce. Add each slice to a pouch, and pour a little sauce over the whole thing. Pull up the edges of the bag around the tempeh, but don't seal. Let this sit on the coolest part of the grill, and rotate (don't flip) occasionally for about 10 to 15 minutes.

For an even easier method, steam the tempeh first for about 20 minutes. I think if you sauté the pieces in the chopped onion and oil, it gives the tempeh a little more flavor. Tempeh cooks so fast on a grill, it doesn't have much time to soak up flavors.

Sauté the onions in some oil in an electric skillet, and add a little of your favorite barbecue sauce. Add the sliced, cooked tempeh, and cover with ½ cup more sauce mixed with about ¼ cup water. Cover and cook at about 275°F to 300°F until it is done the way you like it. Check every 10 minutes or so to see if you need to add more sauce or not. This will depend on your taste, how thick the sauce was, etc. It is easier to control how the tempeh will come out like this. If it is for company and it has to be right, do it like this.

City "Chicken" Legs

Yield: about 10 to 12 legs

1 pound tofu
1 cup cooked chick-peas
1 cup bread crumbs
¼ cup good-tasting nutritional yeast flakes
⅓ cup oatmeal
1 teaspoon thyme
½ cup finely chopped onion
½ cup chopped parsley *(optional)*
2 tablespoons tamari
10 wooden skewers *(Soak in water first.)*
Wild Woman's Bar-Be-Que Sauce, page 72,
   or extra soy margarine or oil for
   brushing
3 tablespoons tamari

Mix all the ingredients together, except the 3 tablespoons tamari, in a bowl, working them together really good with your hands. The mixture should hold together easily.

Gently but firmly press a good bit of the tofu mixture around ½ of a skewer. You may want to rub your hands with oil before you start, as this will make the mixture easier to handle.

If you're cooking these outdoors, brush generously with Wild Woman's Bar-Be-Que Sauce or a bit of melted soy margarine or oil. Place each skewer over the coals, turning and basting them whenever necessary. Don't turn too often.

Here's a tip: When you're cooking tofu over a grill, take it easy—it's not meat, it will fall apart, you have to be gentle. Use common sense—if you keep sticking a fork into these to turn them, they are going to fall apart. Use tongs, be creative.

If you're cooking these indoors, you can do the tofu "legs" with barbecue sauce and bake them in your oven. You can also cover the bottom of a heavy skillet or electric skillet with oil. Roll the legs in flour. (Chick-pea, sesame, or whole wheat flour makes a nice change from regular white, as well as whole sesame seeds.) Place them gently in the hot oil, drizzle over the 3 tablespoons tamari, and fry until crispy on all sides.

Don't use not being able to find skewers as an excuse to not make these; you can always use empty popsicle sticks. Most Oriental markets carry a good selection of skewers.

135

Marinated Grilled Vegetables

Zucchini
Yellow summer squash
Carrots
Broccoli
Cauliflower
Eggplant
Tomato halves
Quartered red peppers

Make a marinade out of one of the recipes that follow, or look in the chapter on salad dressings and find one you like. Slice the vegetables, making them as long as possible so they won't fall through the grill later. Cut the carrots, yellow squash, eggplant, and zucchini lengthwise. Cut the broccoli into spears and the cauliflower into fat flowerettes. Let these marinate for 15 minutes to 1 hour. It is easiest to put the vegetables in a plastic bag along with the dressing, and toss them until well covered. After that, toss them whenever you think of it. Lay these over a medium grill or put in a grill basket for about 10 minutes, or until roasted, brown, and tender.

Tip for vegetables and tofu at a cook-out: There are fabulous grill baskets on the market now shaped like flat woks or cookie sheets. They work great, so if you like to cook out, you should definitely have one in your kitchen. They are not expensive at all, and you will never have to deal with your food falling through the grill again. I can heap mine with peppers, onions, and portobello mushrooms, and it makes a simple and swell dish. Also, this is a delicious way to use up those hundreds of zucchini your garden puts out every summer.

Marinades:

The easiest marinades to make are your favorite oil and vinegar-based salad dressings. Try these variations:

⅓ cup oil
⅓ cup tamari
Juice of ½ lime or lemon *(optional)*

⅓ cup oil
3 tablespoons toasted sesame oil
¼ teaspoon chili powder
A thumb-size piece of fresh ginger finely grated or grated and squeezed to extract the juice (see p. 73), or ¼ teaspoon powdered ginger

⅓ cup oil
¼ cup tamari
1 tablespoon Dijon mustard
1 clove garlic, pressed

Grilled Red Onions and Garlic

Yield: 8 to 10 servings

5 to 6 red onions, Vidalia or whatever
  you have, cut in half
1 to 2 whole garlic bulbs
Your favorite marinade, or
  ¼ to ½ cup olive oil
3 tablespoons tamari
1 tablespoon lemon juice
2 teaspoons thyme
Salt and pepper, to taste

Cut the onions into halves—do not peel. Brush the cut halves with olive oil, or marinate cut side down in the marinade for at least an hour. They will take at least 30 minutes to cook on the grill, but these can cook forever and still be great. They should even be somewhat burnt to taste best. To eat, use the tassels of the onion roots as handles, peel back the skin, and bite in—an onion lollipop!

For the garlic, cut the entire bulb in half, brush with oil, and grill along with the onion. The garlic won't take as long to cook. Put these directly over hot coals, and turn when necessary. You may want to run a toothpick through these, because as they cook they soften and may fall through the grill.

Barbie-Q-Beans

Yield: 10 to 14 servings

This is a delicious recipe and very spicy. It's a good one for any backyard picnic. Of course, this can cook in a pot over a fire, or in the coals of your own fireplace. This would also be a good recipe to add a few pieces of seitan to.

3 to 4 cups dried white, pinto, or lima beans
½ cup molasses
2 onions, sliced
¼ cup prepared mustard
3 tablespoons miso dissolved in ½ cup
  bean cooking water
1 to 2 tablespoons grated ginger
Salt and pepper, to taste
Pinch of allspice
1 tablespoon brown sugar *(This is delicious if you eat sugar, but if not, then it's perfectly fine to omit it.)*

Soak the beans overnight in enough water to cover them. Rinse and cook with enough water to cover for about 2 hours, or until soft.

Preheat the oven to 350°F. Pour off half the water, and mix in the other ingredients. Turn into a deep dish casserole, arrange the onions on top, and bake for 1 hour.

137

Seitan

When was the last time you were at a pot-luck, neighborhood dinner, or the like, and the person sitting next to you looked at you and said, "Do you ever eat Satan?" In the few seconds it takes me to answer, a jillion things run through my head, a few of them being:

1. I'm being recruited by a Satanic cult run by mild-mannered housewives;

2. Quick, grab your big, yellow bowl full of potato salad, and run before you're kidnapped by a Hell's Angel biker group;

3. I should have listened more closely at Sunday School.

It usually takes me a second or two to realize that the person is actually mispronouncing seitan. (It's say-tan, not Satan.) And that yes, I am safe again in my own little world.

Seitan is made from a flour and water dough that has been kneaded until the gluten in the flour has been developed. The ball of dough is then put under running water and kneaded until all the starch and bran is washed away. All that is left is the gluten protein, this great stretchy stuff that is ready to be flavored any way you want and cooked to resemble all sorts of meat or fish, from barbecue to shrimp. When the gluten is cooked, it's called seitan. (Don't ask why—the Japanese have separate names for both the cooked and uncooked stuff.)

If you have never tried making gluten, or wheat meat, from scratch, lucky you. Someone has come along and taken all the work out of it for you. In the old days, I used to make seitan for 40. It took all day to knead this enormous ball of dough (cuz you have to start out with a lot of dough to end up with much gluten), and I had to recruit two friends to help me. (I had to walk to school barefoot in the snow too.) Now you can get the gluten all pre-rinsed in the form of a dry powder—all you have to do is add liquid and flavorings, mix, and you're ready to go. It actually makes seitan feasible as a meal without spending all day and night in the kitchen. It has changed my life. I'll put some information for where to get this on p. 140.

Since you have been a vegetarian, how many times have you heard this phrase or even said it yourself, "Oh, this has no flavor. It will take on the flavor of anything, so you can combine it with almost anything." Have you ever noticed that if you say this to someone who's not familiar with vegetarian cooking, their eyes glaze over? This sentence has done more to set back vegetarianism than any other thing I can think of. People are lost; they have enough trouble cooking—period—much less flavoring the tofu.

Why this rant? Because seitan is one of those things that you have to add flavor to. Fresh tofu at least has a subtle flavor, but seitan pretty much tastes like nothing. (Although, once I made some and didn't flavor it enough, and it tasted like a plate of rubber bands with tomato sauce.) So I'll give you a few good starting recipes; you'll see how good it is. After you make it a few times, you'll get an idea of how you like it—sliced, or with more seasoning, or what. Although I hate recipes that take more than one day to prepare, seitan is one of those things that tastes even better if you let it cook a little one day, let sit in the refrigerator, and finish cooking the next day. Be careful about cooking seitan; it's pure protein with virtually no fat, and sometimes it needs a little bit more oil than you might think.

One good way to make it is by using the fried chicken tofu recipe. This always works well for me. Another good way to get flavor into seitan is flavoring the water you mix it up with or simmer it in, so it can start soaking up flavor as soon as possible. Even if I just use tamari, vegetarian broth powder, onion soup mix, or ketchup, I try to use something to add flavor.

Here's how I mix up seitan using vital wheat gluten or instant gluten flour:

1½ cups vital wheat gluten
1 cup water
¼ cup olive oil, or a combination of olive oil and toasted sesame oil
8 cups vegetable broth

Mix the vital wheat gluten, water, and oil together quickly to make sure all the dry gluten powder is moistened. Knead from 3 to 8 minutes. Divide into 18 to 24 balls, and flatten with the palm of your hand. Don't worry about making them all exactly the same shape. Simmer for about 1 hour in the vegetable broth. Drain and add to your favorite recipe. You can slice or dice the balls to suit your needs.

Bar-B-Que Seitan & Spare Ribs

Yield: 4 to 6 servings

1½ cups vital wheat gluten or instant gluten powder
1 onion, chopped
1 clove garlic, smashed
3 tablespoons tamari
2 tablespoons toasted sesame oil
1 bottle of your favorite barbecue sauce or use a homemade recipe *(You won't need a whole bottle—I'd say about 1½ cups—but everyone likes their barbeque different.)*
Oil, as needed

Prepare the seitan according to the directions on pages 138-39. When the directions say simmer 1 hour, simmer with the chopped onion, garlic, and tamari. Cut the seitan into thin chunks. Don't worry too much about the shape. Layer the chunks in a glass bowl with the barbecue sauce, and let sit in the refrigerator several hours or overnight. I usually let mine cook about 20 to 30 minutes in the electric skillet and put it back in the fridge overnight or all day. You probably won't need any more barbecue sauce, but if you think it looks skimpy, add more, then cover and cook again for as long as possible in the electric skillet until it has that caramelized edge that I will arm wrestle my husband for. If you need to add a bit more sauce mixed with a little bit of water, that's fine.

To make spare ribs: This one is a winner. When shaping the seitan, cut long strips and stretch as long as possible, about 5 or 6 inches. Again, don't worry too much about shape. Let marinate in the barbeque sauce. Use a glass baking dish large enough to accommodate the length of the strips. Use previous directions for layering and marinating in the sauce. When cooking for the second time, bake in the oven for 40 minutes at 350°F. The ribs will tend to get a little tough, which is good because you can pick them up and knaw on them like you would a real rib. Check them after 30 minutes; if they seem too dried out or too hard, you can always just add a little water to the pan, cover, and continue to bake until they soften up.

The Mail Order Catalog (1-800-695-2241) is a good source for all kinds of great fake meat products, including make-your-own seitan.

Stuffed Peppers a la Appalachian

Yield: 6 servings

Stuffed peppers are perfect for picnics because you can make them the day before, they freeze well, they taste better the next day anyway, and you eat the container they come in.

6 large green peppers
¼ cup sesame seeds
2 tablespoons oil
1 onion, chopped
2 carrots, grated
1 clove garlic, finely chopped
½ cup good-tasting nutritional yeast flakes
½ teaspoon dry mustard
Tamari and pepper, to taste
1 pound tofu, diced small
2 cups leftover rice *(Millet, noodles, and any cooked grain will also do.)*

Believe me, if the peppers are not cooked well enough, people will just eat the stuffing and throw the peppers away. Barely slice the top off each pepper, and reserve. Scoop out the pulp and seeds, and throw away. Put the peppers cut side down in a pan with just a little water. Steam until they turn bright green, then remove from the heat and leave covered until you need them. This just takes a few minutes.

Heat the sesame seeds in the oil until they start to pop, then add the onions, carrots, garlic, nutritional yeast, mustard, and tamari and pepper to taste. Cook until the vegetables are tender but not done.

Preheat the oven to 350°F. Add the diced tofu to the simmering vegetables. Then add everything to the leftover rice, and mix up real good. Stuff into the steamed peppers. Put these upright in a casserole dish. Some people like a slice of cheese on top, but I like a dot of soy margarine with bread crumbs.

If you want, put a pan of water in the bottom of the oven so these can steam. Bake about 30 minutes.

Roasted Corn

10 ears of corn with the husks still on

Pull back the tops of the husks, and remove the silk. Put the husks back up, and soak the ears in salted water for 5 minutes. Grill over hot coals for about 10 to 15 minutes. Turn these frequently. If you find your grill is filled up with burgers and shish-ke-bobs, and there is no room for the corn, don't worry. You can pile it in your oven and roast it for 20 to 25 minutes at 400°F.

Granny's Best "Cheese" Sandwich

Yield: 6 sandwiches

These sandwiches are so good that every time I made them for Patsy, Dori, and me, we ate them all before we got out of town. You can't get a better traveling sandwich; it gets better as it sits. I get mine out early and put it on the dashboard to kind of "heat up." This recipe is a winner; it sounds too easy to be this good, but it is.

½ pound sharp cheddar or soy cheddar cheese
¼ to ½ cup mayonnaise, depending on your taste
One small onion, grated *(It may be easier to hold if you get a big onion and grate about half of it in)*
Salt and pepper, to taste
Bread, as needed

Grate the cheese into a bowl, mix in the mayo, grate in the onion, and add the salt and pepper. Spread generously on bread. I like thinly sliced or extra-thinly sliced Pepperidge Farm. Enjoy in any picnic lunch or road trip.

Katy-Did Special Sandwich

Yield: 4 sandwiches

I listed all the ingredients that I like on this sandwich, but it's just as good with only avocado, mayo, and sesame salt. This is also a great sandwich to grill.

2 avocados, peeled and thinly sliced
1 tomato, sliced *(if you like tomato)*
Sesame salt, as needed*
Mayonnaise
Dijon mustard
2 tablespoons crumbled blue cheese
(optional)
Pita or sliced whole wheat bread *(Really, any bread works well, but you get more to eat if you use pita.)*

*Here's how to make sesame salt: Toast about 1 cup sesame seeds over a low flame in a cast-iron skillet; you'll be able to smell them. If they start popping, you have the flame turned up too high; turn it down a little. I like to let mine get real dark—not burnt, just well roasted. When the sesame seeds are about half done, add about 2 teaspoons salt. There are many theories about how much salt to use; some say 1 part salt to 16 parts seeds. I don't know what this works out to, but I know I don't like mine too salty. After you make this once, you'll know how you like it. Let the salt and seeds finish cooking together. You can grind this in a blender until it looks like course salt or do it by hand in a suribachi (one of those little bowls with grooves in the bottom). Sesame salt will keep in an airtight container. It's one of my favorite condiments. Try it on sandwiches, popcorn, soup, toast, muffins, bagels, baked potatoes, baked squash, noodles, rice, salad, and sushi. It tastes like bacon bits.

Tofu "Cold Chicken" Sandwich

Yield: 1 to 2 sandwiches

This sandwich is so good, I really encourage you to try this recipe. The only hard part is that everyone, including me, likes "chicken" fried tofu so much, there's never any leftover. Maybe you should make twice the amount. If you are eating this at home for lunch, add a slice of homegrown tomato.

Bread *(especially Pepperidge Farm X-Thin Sliced Whole Wheat for picnics)*
Mayonnaise
Very thinly sliced raw red onion
2 to 4 slices leftover "chicken" fried tofu
(This has to be leftover in the fridge for at least one night.)

Toast the bread if you want, and spread with mayonnaise. Add the sliced onion, tomato, and tofu.

Ed-Ray's Scotch Blondies

Yield: 12 to 14

This is my easiest cookie recipe and my favorite. I love it because you don't have to let the margarine come to room temperature, so the cookies are done faster. And you only get one pot dirty, which is a big plus to me.

½ cup soy margarine
1¼ cups brown sugar
2 eggs or egg replacer
1 teaspoon vanilla
1¼ cups flour
½ teaspoon baking powder
¼ teaspoon salt
1 cup pecan pieces

Preheat the oven to 350°F. Melt the margarine in a saucepan. Remove from the heat and stir in the sugar, egg replacer, and vanilla. In a separate bowl, mix the flour, baking powder, and salt. Stir into the margarine-sugar mixture. Grease a 9 x 9-inch baking dish, and pour or press the batter into the dish. Sprinkle with the chopped pecans. Bake for 25 to 30 minutes, or until golden brown. Cool on a rack before cutting.

Breads

A crust eaten in peace is better than a banquet partaken in anxiety.

Aesop

Bread is the warmest, kindest of words. Write it always with a capital letter, like your own name.

Russian Cafe Sign

Kitty Sue's Cinnamon Coconut Rolls

Yield: 3 to 4 servings

This is a wonderful recipe, because no matter what kind of cook you are, or what time of the day or night it is, you'll probably have these ingredients sitting around your kitchen.

Topping:
½ cup honey or brown sugar
¼ cup soy margarine, softened
⅔ cup grated coconut
Dash of cinnamon

1¾ cups plus 2 tablespoons flour
2 teaspoons baking powder
½ teaspoon salt
¼ cup soy margarine

¾ cup milk or soymilk

Preheat the oven to 425°F. Combine the ingredients for the topping in a small bowl, and set aside.

To make the rolls, combine the flour, baking powder, and salt in a medium bowl. Cut the margarine into the dry ingredients until it's the size of peas. Add the milk slowly until the dough is moist. Turn out and knead for 20 seconds, then pat the dough into a rectangle. Spread the topping mixture in the bottom of a 8-inch square baking pan, and place the dough (or piece if you have to) over the top. Bake for about 20 minutes or until done. Remove from the oven and cut into squares. Don't leave this in the pan to remove later; it sticks. Lift out with a spatula, and serve upside down on serving plates. You'll feel just like Betty Crocker.

Blue Ribbon Blueberry Muffins

Yield: 1 dozen

¼ cup soft soy margarine
½ cup honey
1 egg
¾ cup milk or soymilk
¼ teaspoon vanilla
1¾ cups white or whole wheat flour
2½ teaspoons baking powder
½ teaspoon salt
1 cup blueberries

Preheat the oven to 425°F. In a medium bowl, cream the margarine and honey, then beat in the egg, milk, and vanilla. In a small bowl, stir together flour, baking powder, and salt. Add to the wet mixture and stir. The combined mixture will be moist and a little lumpy. Mix about a tablespoon of flour with the berries, and fold into the batter. Spoon into greased muffin tins, and bake for 25 minutes, or until evenly golden brown.

Sarah's Prize Winners

Yield: about 10 to 12 muffins

My grandmother won first prize in a contest with this recipe. After you try them, you'll know why.

1¼ cups buttermilk, sour milk, or soymilk
1 cup whole bran
¼ cup soy margarine
⅓ cup honey
1 egg or egg replacer
1½ cups whole wheat flour
1½ teaspoons baking powder
½ teaspoon salt
¼ teaspoon baking soda
1 cup grated cheddar cheese

Preheat the oven to 400°F. Pour the buttermilk over the bran, and let it sit until the mixture is soft. Cream the honey, margarine, and egg in a separate bowl. Mix the dry ingredients, then add the creamed mixture alternately with the milk-bran mixture. Stir in the grated cheese. Grease muffin tins and fill ⅔ full with batter. Bake for about 30 minutes.

Buttermilk Biscuits

Yield: 12 to 14

2 cups flour *(Use white or whole wheat in any combination; just remember, the lighter the flour, the lighter the biscuits.)*
2½ teaspoons baking powder
½ teaspoon salt
¼ teaspoon baking soda
¾ cup buttermilk
1 tablespoon honey
5 tablespoons melted soy margarine

Preheat the oven to 450°F. Mix the dry ingredients in a bowl, and make a well in the center. Pour in the buttermilk, honey, and melted margarine. **This is the tricky part.** Stir with as few strokes as possible, just until the dough follows the fork around the bowl. Too much stirring will make your biscuits like little rocks. Turn the dough out onto a floured board, and knead gently about 6 times, just to help it take shape. Roll this out with a rolling pin, handling as little as possible, to about ¼ to ½ inch thick. Cut with a biscuit cutter, being careful not to twist the cutter. Put the biscuits on a greased cookie sheet, and bake 10 to 15 minutes.

Shady Side Nut Muffins

Yield: 1 dozen

If you want a sweeter muffin to use as a dessert or for tea, add ½ cup raisins or a chopped apple.

1¼ cups whole wheat flour
½ cup any other flour *(oat, rye, buckwheat, soy, etc.)*
2 teaspoons baking powder
½ teaspoon salt
¼ cup each of 3 kinds of chopped nuts *(You can use sesame seeds, walnuts, sliced or toasted almonds, pumpkin seeds, cashews, peanuts, etc.)*
1 cup water or soymilk
1 egg or egg replacer
3 tablespoons oil
2 tablespoons honey or sugar

Preheat the oven to 350°F. Mix the flours, baking powder, and salt together, and add the nuts and raisins or apple, if using.

Stir together the milk or water, egg, oil, and honey. Pour this into the dry ingredients all at once, and stir until moist. Grease muffin tins and fill ¾ full with batter. Bake for 20 minutes. Serve hot for dinner or spread with jam for dessert.

Granny's Banana Bread

Yield: 12 muffins, 1 large loaf, or 2 small loaves

The secret of this recipe is to cream the wet ingredients as smoothly as possible. Use an electric mixer if you have one, or even a food processor. The smoother the batter, the lighter your bread will be, so get those ingredients mixed up real well. This recipe also makes good muffins, so don't just cook it always as one long loaf.

¼ cup soy margarine
½ cup sugar
3 eggs or egg replacer
3 mashed bananas *(the riper, the better)*
⅓ cup water mixed with 3 tablespoons
    milk or soymilk
1 teaspoon vanilla
1 teaspoon salt
2 teaspoons baking powder
1 teaspoon baking soda
2 cups flour *(white, whole wheat, or a
    combination)*
¼ cup wheat germ
¾ to 1 cup walnuts or pecans
½ cup raisins

Preheat the oven to 350°F. Cream the margarine and honey in a medium bowl, then mix in the eggs or egg replacer, mashed bananas, and water/milk mixture. Mix the dry ingredients and, with as few strokes as possible, blend them into the banana-honey mixture. Stir in the nuts and raisins. Pour the batter into a greased loaf pan. This is a pretty heavy bread; don't use a real deep pan, or your bread will never get done in the middle. You can also put it in small loaf pans. Bake for 1 hour, or until a straw or toothpick comes out clean.

Hushpuppies

Yield: 12 to 15

At any Southern outdoor to-do, there are bound to be dogs, and where there are dogs, there most assuredly are a few puppies. The hounds would start to fuss, the pups would follow, and the cooks, with no other choice, would fling bits of batter left from a deep-fry with a plea, "hush, puppy!"

I like to make these with tempeh, frying both at the same time. Hushpuppies are a great change from cornbread, and they go real well with vegetables. How about boiled potatoes, collard greens, and hushpuppies for dinner tonight? They are also as good with ketchup as they are with tartar sauce.

Enough oil to deep-fry *(peanut is good)*
2 cups cornmeal
1 teaspoon baking powder
½ teaspoon baking soda
1 egg or egg replacer
1 tablespoon honey
1 cup buttermilk or sour soymilk
Dash of cayenne
1 teaspoon salt
¼ to ½ cup finely chopped green onions
⅛ teaspoon garlic powder
1 tablespoon grated onion

Mix the cornmeal, baking powder, and baking soda in a medium bowl, and make a well in the center. Stir the buttermilk, egg, and honey together in a small bowl, and pour into the well. Stir and add the onions. Drop this mixture by spoonfuls into hot oil (375°F), and fry until golden.

Hoecakes

Yield: 8 to 10

These cakes may be baked on a griddle, just as you would a griddle cake, and served with soy margarine. But old Southern cooks always baked them on a hoe on hot coals in front of the fire out in the open air in front of their cabin doors, or in their cabin before a roaring fire. Hence the name "hoecake." The term hoecake, so extensively used by field hands, was taken up by cooks in general and applied to the biscuit bread described below.

This recipe came from one of my favorite cookbooks, River Road Recipes. *It's full of things one couldn't live without, such as "Salad for 70." The whole recipe is 18 heads of lettuce and 8 bunches parsley. It's a great book and will provide hours of entertainment.*

Hoecakes as made at the "Big House":
2 cups flour
1 cup milk
1 teaspoon yeast
2 tablespoons soy margarine

Hoecakes as made in the "Cabin":
1 teaspoon shortening
2 cups flour
1 teaspoon salt
Enough boiling water to make a batter

Preheat the oven to 375°F. Mix the ingredients well and knead for a minute. Roll the dough out with a rolling pin, cut criss-cross with a knife, like diamonds. Place on an ungreased cookie sheet, and bake for 20 minutes.

Crispy Garlic Skillet Cornbread

Read the flawless cornbread recipe on p. 37 in the chapter on East Tennessee Favorites. You make this the same way, only the beginning is different. One night my husband said to me, "Will you put some garlic in the cornbread?" I figured I would just cut up a bunch and put it in the batter, and then I had one of those brief flashes of genius in my pea-sized brain. I cut up a lot of elephant garlic, about 4 or 5 cloves (you can't use too much), and put it in the skillet with the soy margarine to heat in the oven while I made the batter. When the margarine was melted, I made sure the garlic was spread evenly over the bottom of the skillet, and then poured the batter over it and baked as usual.

If you are a garlic lover, watch out— you'll have a new addiction with this recipe. The garlic gets that golden, crusty, caramelized crunch, and with the margarine dripping down, the subtle sweet of the white corn, . . . this should be called "better than sex" cornbread.

Rock Fork Drop Biscuits

Yield: 8 large or 12 small

This is a good biscuit to make when you are in a hurry; you don't have to roll them out.

1½ cups whole wheat flour
1¼ cups white flour or soy flour
¼ to ½ cup wheat germ *(optional)*
1 tablespoon baking powder
1 teaspoon salt
5 to 6 tablespoons oil *(Safflower or sesame is good.)*
1¼ cups soymilk, milk, or half water and half milk

Preheat the oven to 400°F. Stir the dry ingredients together in a bowl, and cut in the oil. Add the milk all at once, and stir quickly until blended. Drop teaspoonfuls onto a greased cookie sheet. Bake for about 12 to 15 minutes until nice and brown on the bottom. Serve hot with any soup, beans, lots of gravy, breakfast, soy margarine, honey, and jam with tea.

Coffee Ridge Pineapple Nut Bread

Yield: 1 large loaf or 2 small loaves

This is a very rich loaf, more like cake than bread. It has a real holiday feel to it and can be made in advance to age as a gift under someone's tree.

2¼ cups whole wheat or white flour
1 cup wheat bran or wheat germ
2 teaspoons baking powder
1¼ teaspoons salt
1 teaspoon baking soda
¾ cup honey
3 tablespoons oil or melted soy margarine
1 egg or egg replacer
1½ cups very finely chopped pineapple
2 tablespoons pineapple juice
1 teaspoon vanilla, or 1 teaspoon rum extract
1 cup chopped pecans or walnuts
½ to 1 cup dark raisins

Preheat the oven to 350°F. Stir the dry ingredients together. In another bowl, mix the honey, oil, egg replacer, pineapple, pineapple juice, and rum or vanilla extract. Add this to the dry ingredients, then stir in the nuts and raisins. If it seems dry, add a little more pineapple juice. Bake in a greased loaf pan for 1 to 1¼ hours. A straw or toothpick should come out clean when the bread is done.

After it cools (best to sit it on a wire rack), wrap it well in plastic wrap, then aluminum foil, and let it sit and mellow for 3 to 10 days.

Short'nin Bread

Yield: 8 to 10 servings

When I made this at work one day, my friend Tina came rushing into the kitchen. "These taste just like what my neighbor in Boston, Mrs. Jamison, used to make. When she gave me the recipe, she told me it was handed down in her family since the last great-great-grandmother that anyone could remember; she called it Scotch short bread."

On close inspection, we discovered that Mrs. Jamison used rice flour and I used whole wheat, but we both cut diamonds across the top. Tina and I both got off on wondering where this recipe might first have sprung up, but the fact that it's so widely loved and simply made is reason enough for you to try it.

2 cups flour (rice, whole wheat, or any
    combination)
½ teaspoon salt
1 cup soy margarine, softened *(Old time
    recipes say don't substitute margarine
    for butter, but I always do.)*
½ cup brown sugar, or ¼ cup
    plus 2 tablespoons honey, rice syrup,
    molasses, maple syrup, or barley malt
1 teaspoon vanilla *(optional)*

Preheat the oven to 350°F. Combine the flour, brown sugar, and salt in a bowl. (If you're using liquid sweetener, add it after you cut in the margarine.) Cut the margarine into chunks, and cut it into the flour mixture with a pastry blender or 2 sharp knives. You want to do this until it's like cornmeal. If you're using liquid sweetener, add it now with a fork until it becomes very smooth—it shouldn't take too long. Place the dough on an ungreased cookie sheet or baking pan, and press down with your fingers. Cut diamonds into the top of the dough, and prick with a fork. Bake for about 20 minutes, or until the shortbread is light brown and starts to pull slightly away from the edge of the pan.

Mom's Dining Room Refrigerator Rolls

Yield: 3 dozen

The best thing about these rolls is that they're easy and so good I've seen people eat eight or nine at one sitting. I always make these when I don't have time to fool around in the kitchen before a party. Since the batter rises in the refrigerator, you can mix them up the day before and have the biggest part done early.

Once when I was making these, our refrigerator blew up (not due to the rolls), so I just put the dough on the back porch in a big snowstorm, and it worked just fine. You don't have to leave it overnight—4 hours at least and 2 days at the most.

If, perchance, you have any of these left over, they're great toasted for breakfast with jam and tea.

½ cup soy margarine
¼ cup honey
1 teaspoon salt
½ cup boiling water
1 egg or egg replacer
1 package or tablespoon baking yeast
1 cup warm water
3 to 4 cups flour *(You can use any combination of white or whole wheat flour in these rolls—100% whole wheat works fine.)*
¼ cup soy margarine, melted

Place the margarine, honey, and salt in a medium bowl, and pour the boiling water over. Blend and let cool. Add the egg or egg replacer. Dissolve the yeast in the warm water, and let sit for about 5 minutes, then add the activated yeast to the rest of the mixture. Mix in the flour with about 200 strokes. Put in a well-greased bowl, and place in the refrigerator with a damp cloth on top.

About 3 hours before needed, take the dough out of the refrigerator (or out of the cold), and let it sit for about 20 minutes. (If you try to work with it right away, it'll be too hard to handle.) Roll the dough to about ¼ inch thick. Cut out circles in the dough with a biscuit cutter or a wide-mouth jar or glass at least 2 inches across. Dip one flat side of each piece into the melted margarine, and fold over, margarine side in. Place these close together on a cookie sheet, and brush the tops lightly with the remaining margarine. Let them sit about 2 hours. Bake at 425°F for 12 to 15 minutes, or until the bottoms are browned.

Easy Overnight Cinnamon Rolls

Yield: 24 large or 36 small rolls

This is a good recipe for someone who is really serious about having cinnamon rolls for breakfast. Most of the work is done the day or night before, and you can finish them while you are wandering around making coffee the next morning. I like to use this recipe, otherwise my cinnamon rolls aren't ready before suppertime.

Okay, use the recipe from Mom's Refrigerator Rolls on p. 155. Go ahead and put the dough in the fridge, just like it says. The next morning take it out and let it sit about 20 minutes, so it will be workable. Roll it out into a big rectangle about ¼ to ½ inch thick.

Spread with soft soy margarine (add to suit yourself.) Sprinkle with brown sugar or drizzle with honey (lots). Add some chopped nuts. Sprinkle with about 1 tablespoon cinnamon.

Roll up like a jelly roll, then take a sharp knife and slice off 1-inch sections. Place in a greased casserole, fairly close together but not touching. Brush with a little more margarine or honey, if you want. Cover and let rise about ½ to 1 hour until doubled. Bake at 375°F for 15 to 20 minutes, until golden and done. If the smell of coffee and cinnamon rolls doesn't get everyone out of bed, nothing will.

Sweets

*The black stove, stoked with coal and firewood,
glowed like a lighted pumpkin. Egg beaters whirl,
spoons spin round in bowls of butter and sugar,
vanilla sweetens the air, ginger spices it; melting,
nose-tingling odors saturate the kitchen, suffuse the
house, drift out to the world on puffs of chimney
smoke. In four days our work is done. Thirty-one
cakes, dampened with whiskey, bask on window sills
and shelves.*

Truman Capote,
A Christmas Memory

*I am weary of swords and courts and kings. Let us
go into the garden and watch the minister's bees.*
Mary Johnston

Aprons

I waited until the end of this book to lecture you, and now it's time. Do you have your apron on, and if not, why? The apron is the most under-used, misunderstood item in your kitchen, if you even have one in your kitchen.

There is nothing a good apron can't do. Why, last week my apron helped to avert a robbery. As I swept into Davis' Filling Station, in a cloud of flour and cinnamon, I was still wearing my favorite apron (the one with the poodles, martini glasses, and cherry bombs). Little did I know that a bunch of young hoodlums had just threatened Sam. They took one look at me, half covered in flour, apron blazing, and were so taken aback, they dropped everything and ran off to rob someone else. Sam still laughs about this and swears I ought to give some aprons to the county sheriff.

I have come to the conclusion that there is just something goddess-like about wearing an apron. Who could hurt someone wearing an apron? It's almost always a sign that there's a baby, a grandmother, or something good to eat nearby. Not even the worst of criminals would bop his grandmother on the head.

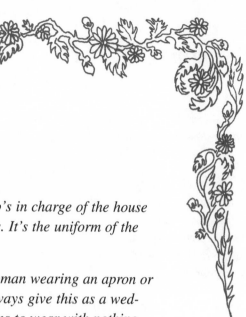

Aprons have been a sign of who's in charge of the house for as long as we've lived in houses. It's the uniform of the kitchen, best room of the house.

There's nothing as sexy as a woman wearing an apron or wearing nothing but an apron. I always give this as a wedding shower gift with the instructions to wear with nothing but high heels as soon as you feel the honeymoon is starting to wear off.

I've discovered I seem to wander around the kitchen accomplishing nothing until I get my apron on, and that's when things really get cooking. So if you don't have a good apron, you have been warned. Don't cook another thing without it.

Swannanoa Shortcake

Yield: 8 to 10 servings

This shortcake whips up very fast and is good to have with any fruit in season. I like to use peaches, blueberries, or blackberries.

2 cups flour
3 teaspoons baking powder
1 teaspoon salt
⅓ cup soy margarine
1 cup milk or soymilk
2 tablespoons sugar

Preheat the oven to 400°F. Mix the dry ingredients together, then cut in the margarine until it becomes the consistency of cornmeal. Stir in the milk all at once quickly, until just blended. Press into a either an 8 x 8-inch or 9 x 13-inch greased pan (depending on how thick you want your shortcake to be). Dot with margarine and bake for 12 to 15 minutes. Cut into nice-sized squares, and serve with your favorite fruit. Strawberries, pineapple, blackberries, raspberries, or peaches are all good.

Fruit Glaze

Yield: about 1 cup

If you miss whipped cream and want something to pour over your shortcake, here is a good fruit glaze.

½ to 1 cup fruit
1 tablespoon honey
1 teaspoon kudzu
¼ cup cold water

Smash the fruit with a potato masher, just until it starts to ooze juice a little. Put in a saucepan with the honey. Dissolve the kudzu in the cold water, and add to the fruit. Stir over medium heat until thickened. Let cool and serve over any shortcake.

Great Aunt Alzenia's Brownies

Yield: 8 large or 12 small

This is a great recipe for a small batch of brownies. If you want a lot or even just a big pan, you can double or triple this recipe.

½ cup soy margarine

¾ cup sugar

3 squares unsweetened chocolate,
   or 3 tablespoons cocoa or carob

2 eggs or egg replacer

1 teaspoon vanilla

¼ teaspoon salt

¾ cup flour

¼ teaspoon baking powder

1 cup chopped walnuts or pecans

Preheat the oven to 350°F. Melt the margarine in a saucepan, and add the sugar and chocolate or cocoa (or whatever you're using). Remove from the heat and let cool a few minutes. Quickly stir in the eggs, vanilla, and salt, then fold in the flour, baking powder, and nuts. Don't stir this too much, but make sure it's smooth. Pour in a greased 8-inch square pan, and bake about 30 minutes.

This is one recipe where the toothpick test doesn't really work. I like brownies chewy, so after about 25 minutes, I take them out of the oven and check them. Press your finger lightly to the middle. You'll know if it's too gooey and not done; it'll be gummy still. The brownies should be about done by then, but if you have to leave them in another 5 minutes, go ahead. Be sure not to overbake them though, as they will become dried out. When you take them out, let them sit about 30 minutes before you cut them.

Mamma's Dark Secret

Yield: 10 to 12 servings

2 cups unbleached white flour
1 teaspoon salt
1 cup soy margarine
4 tablespoons cocoa or carob
1 cup coffee
1½ cups white or brown sugar
2 eggs or egg replacer
½ cup buttermilk
1 teaspoon vanilla
1 teaspoon baking soda

Frosting:

½ cup soy margarine
4 tablespoons cocoa
6 tablespoons milk
1 teaspoon vanilla
½ cup honey
1 to 1½ cups powdered milk or soymilk
1½ cups chopped toasted pecans
½ cup chopped almonds *(optional)*

Preheat the oven to 350°F. Stir the flour and salt together in a bowl. Put the margarine, cocoa, and coffee in a saucepan, and bring just to a boil. Stir in the honey. When the honey is dissolved, pour all this over the dry ingredients, and mix well. Beat in the eggs, buttermilk, and vanilla. Add the soda last. Pour into a greased and floured 10 x 15-inch pan or two 9-inch pie plates. Bake for 30 minutes or until a straw or toothpick comes out clean when stuck in the middle.

While the cake is baking, make the frosting. Bring the margarine, cocoa, and milk just to boiling. Remove from the heat and add the vanilla and honey. Stir in the powdered milk with a whip; add it slowly to make sure it doesn't lump. Stir in the toasted pecans and almonds, if you're using them. Pour this over the cake while the cake is still hot. Mamma tells me this is the secret.

Prissy's Easy
Peach Cobbler

Yield: 6 to 8 servings

This cobbler is the greatest! You assemble it in layers without stirring, and the batter poofs up and makes a golden brown topping. It also works on most any fruit; I've used berries, apples, blueberries, etc. Frozen fruit will also do in a pinch.

¼ cup soy margarine
1 cup unbleached white or whole wheat flour
¾ cup sugar
Pinch of salt
1 tablespoon baking powder
⅔ cup milk or soymilk
5 cups sliced fresh peaches *(or enough to generously cover the pan)*
Grated fresh lemon peel
¼ teaspoon cinnamon
¼ teaspoon cloves

Preheat the oven to 350°F. Melt the margarine and pour it into an oblong casserole dish or what have you. Mix the dry ingredients together, and add the milk or soymilk. Stir up really well. Pour into the casserole dish on top of the margarine. Remember—don't stir this. Add the sliced peaches and any juice they've rendered. I'll tell you again, don't stir this! Sprinkle the grated lemon peel over everything. (You can even grate the lemon peel over the pan to make it easier.) Sprinkle the cinnamon and cloves on top of that. Bake for 40 minutes, or until the top is golden brown.

Susan's Apple Crisp

Yield: two 9 x 13-inch pans
(recipe can be cut in half)

Once, in leaner times, Susan and Patsy both had jobs as waitresses at a place called Allen's Harem Lounge. It specialized in hot soups and Allen's Famous Cornbread. Since Allen spent most of his time at his bookie's, most of the responsibility for running the place was left to Marge. She was the kind of lady who ran an hour and a half late on a good day, so things could get a little out of hand at the Harem Lounge.

Marge would usually get to work about 5 minutes before the first customer showed up. She would race around like a maniac, her apron on, ladle in one hand, a Kool extra long in the other, shouting orders like, "Quick, chop 12 onions" or "I need 2 bunches of parsley minced." Of course, as soon as you tried to chop the onions, Marge would run by again frantically and say, "What are you doing that for? Hurry up and make the apple crisp!"

Marge always swore that Susan made the best apple crisp of anyone who ever worked there. So here it is from the Harem Lounge via Susan— apple crisp. This recipe will make a lot—enough for your family and a neighbor's too, or a big pot luck, or a picnic. If you don't need this much, just cut it in half. Susan says tart apples work the best, but she usually used whatever Marge got on sale at the nearest grocery store

6 pounds apples, cut and peeled *(if you want)*
2 teaspoons cinnamon
1 cup brown sugar, or ¾ cup honey

Mix the apples with the cinnamon and brown sugar, and place in a baking dish. Be sure to use a glass dish and not a metal one. (Metal will discolor the apples).

You have three choices for the topping. To 2 cups brown sugar or 1½ cups honey, add:

1. 2 cups whole wheat flour
   2 cups soy margarine
   Pinch salt

2. 1 cup whole wheat flour
   1 cup oats
   2 cups soy margarine

3. 1 cup whole wheat flour
   ½ cup oats
   ½ cup wheat germ
   2 cups soy margarine

Mix together one of these topping mixtures with your hands until it's crumbly. To this, add the brown sugar or honey, and keep mixing. Pack this down on the apples, and bake—the cooking time is debatable. Susan said she would make the crisp, put it in the oven, and start waiting on tables. Midway through the first lunch rush, she would see Marge drop whatever she was doing and run wildly to the kitchen, nose to the air, sniffing like a bloodhound. "Ahhhh, get the apple crisp—it's going to burn!" Usually it never burned; it was done just about the time the first customer was ready for dessert. Susan says estimate it at about 45 to 50 minutes at 350°F.

Cupid's Thumbprints

Yield: 18 cookies

These cookies are exquisite and look beautiful on a plate. They are very fancy little cookies.

½ cup soy margarine
2 tablespoons brown sugar*
3 tablespoons honey or maple syrup
1 egg or egg replacer
½ teaspoon vanilla
1 cup flour
¼ teaspoon salt
½ teaspoon baking soda
¼ to ½ cup sesame seeds
Red raspberry or strawberry jam

Preheat the oven to 350°F. Mix the margarine, sweeteners, egg, and vanilla until smooth. In another bowl, mix all the dry ingredients, except the sesame seeds, then add to the wet ingredients. Be careful not to over-stir. Roll a spoonful of dough into a ball, and roll in sesame seeds. Place 1 inch apart on an ungreased cookie sheet, and press your thumb into the center of each ball. Bake for 10 to 12 minutes, or until brown on the bottom. Fill with red raspberry or strawberry jam.

*If you don't use brown sugar, use a total of ⅓ cup of honey or maple syrup.

Chocolate Chip Cookies

Yield: about 3 dozen

I LOVE chocolate chip cookies. I could even eat them for breakfast, and have done so on many occasions. This is a fool-proof recipe. These cookies turn out like a really sweet bread; we jokingly call them muffin cookies. This is also a good recipe to experiment with.

1 cup soft soy margarine

¾ cup white or brown sugar *(If you don't use sugar, substitute 1 cup honey.)*

1 teaspoon vanilla

2 eggs or egg replacer

2¼ cups whole wheat or unbleached white flour

1 teaspoon baking soda

1 teaspoon salt

1 cup chopped walnuts or pecans *(or your favorite nuts)*

One 24-ounce package semi-sweet chocolate chips or carob chips

Preheat the oven to 350°F. In a large bowl, cream the margarine and sweetener. Make sure this is smooth and not lumpy. Whip in the vanilla and eggs until smooth. In a smaller bowl, mix together the flour, soda, and salt, and add this to the creamed mixture. Stir in the nuts and chocolate chips. Drop on an ungreased cookie sheet, and bake about 10 minutes, until brown on the bottom.

At the warehouse, it never mattered what kind of cookie I made. Someone would wander into the kitchen and say, "Hey, why don't these have any chocolate chips in them?"

At first, I gave what I considered to be a normal response, like, "Well, these are carrot-raisin cookies," or "These are apple-apricot cookies." Later, I learned that to most people, a cookie just isn't a cookie without chocolate chips. When in Rome, . . . soon I was dumping bags of chocolate chips into everything, no matter what the recipe. Here are some of the variations that have worked for me.

1. Add 1½ cups oatmeal and 1½ cups raisins to the original recipe.

2. Cream ½ to 1 cup peanut butter with the margarine and honey in the original recipe. Or substitute peanuts for the walnuts, or just use crunchy peanut butter and forget about the nuts altogether.

3. Add 1 cup coconut to the original recipe.

4. Once I was in a hurry and didn't have time to cream the honey and margarine by hand, so I melted it on the stove real fast. When I mixed it all up together, it was still warm and started to melt the chips. I was afraid they would turn out yucky, but the cookies were delicious—a dark, rich, brown with tiny bits of chips left inside. I got more comments on these cookies; everyone loved them.

5. If I have a little coffee left over, I go ahead and pour it in when I'm creaming the honey and margarine.

6. Substitute 2 tablespoons Kaluha, Jack Daniels, amaretto, or whatever liquor you like for the vanilla.

7. One to 1½ cups any dry cereal you have on hand (Rice Crispies, corn flakes, Wheaties, bran flakes) added to the dry ingredients will make a very crunchy cookie.

8. If you're in a big hurry, just spread all the cookie batter in the bottom of a pie plate or casserole dish, and bake like a bar cookie.

Seven-Layer Cookies or Magic Cookie Bars

Yield:12 to 15

Whenever people sit around and talk about their favorite sweet thing, somebody will bring this one up. It is one of the easiest and most loved.

½ cup soy margarine
1½ cups graham cracker crumbs
One 14-ounce can condensed milk
1 cup chopped nuts
One 6-ounce package semi-sweet
    chocolate chips
1 cup shredded coconut

This is real easy and done in layers—don't stir it up! Preheat the oven to 350°F. Melt the margarine and pour it into a 9 x 13-inch pan. Spread the graham cracker crumbs next, then the nuts, chocolate chips, and coconut. Pour the condensed milk over the whole thing. (I've also used milk thickened with cornstarch and lots of honey before.) Cook in the oven for 30 minutes. Let cool and cut into small squares—these are intense and very addictive. Tina likes to keep hers in the refrigerator.

Cranberry Frappe and How to Make Sherbet

Yield: fifteen ½-cup servings

This is a delightful dessert and quite a surprise. It is a MUST with any big Thanksgiving or Christmas to-do. It has been a tradition in my family since 1903 when my great-grandmother Jenny Hunter served it at her china wedding anniversary. I love to make sherbet, and I also love to eat it. I've also made this with strawberries, blackberries, raspberries, and pineapple. These fruits don't take as much sugar as cranberries do; I'd say you'll only need about ¼ to ½ cup sweetener. You can also use soymilk or buttermilk for half the amount of liquid in all sherbets but the cranberry.

You've also heard me mention Lakewood Peaches and Cream, Strawberries and Cream, coconut milk, and lots of other fruit drinks—all dairy-free. These are great to use as half the liquid in any sherbet. They also work in coconut cream pie, banana pudding, or in any icing.

1 pound fresh cranberries
4 cups water
2¼ cups sugar
Juice of 2 lemons

Cook the berries in the water very slowly until soft. Mash them through a sieve or colander. Add sugar to the juice, and stir until completely dissolved. When cool, add the lemon juice. Pour in a big bowl, and freeze until it's thick like hard mush. Remove and beat with an electric beater until light and fluffy. Freeze again to a hard mush, then remove and beat with the mixer again. (All this freezing and mixing keeps ice crystals from forming.) Store in cartons in the freezer, and keep frozen until ready to serve. The secret of this recipe is to mix it 3 or 4 times.

War Cake: Eggless, Butterless, and Milkless

Yield: 12 to 15 servings

I got this recipe from an old cookbook put out by a Ladies Trinity Mission. The recipe dates back to the Civil War and was not given away, but sold for ten cents to benefit the Red Cross. This version of the recipe includes my own slight variations. I love old recipes like this one! It reminds me of something that Miss Mellie Hamilton would serve at the weekly meeting of the Association for the Beautification of the Graves of Our Glorious Dead.

2 cups brown sugar or 1½ cups honey
2 cups hot water
2 teaspoons soy margarine or corn oil
1 package sultana raisins *(I use however many I have around)*
1 teaspoon salt
1 teaspoon cinnamon
1 teaspoon cloves
3 cups flour
1 teaspoon soda dissolved in a tiny bit of hot water

Preheat the oven to 300°F. Bring the sugar, hot water, margarine, raisins, salt, and spices to a boil, and continue to cook for 5 minutes. When cool, add the flour and soda. Place in a greased 9 x 13-inch baking pan, and bake for 45 minutes. When it's cooled, wrap in aluminum foil. This cake improves by keeping.

Agar-Agar

Yield: *If you tell people this is agar-agar, no one will eat it; if you can keep it a secret, it will serve 6 to 8.*

The first time I ever heard of this stuff, I thought, "I may be dumb, but I'm not stupid, . . . It'll be a long time before I make anything to eat out of something called agar-agar." After I saw what it looked like, it was even easier to ignore. I mean really, long sticks of seaweed? Agar-agar? Jello? No way. I went on stubbornly for years.

One day this girl wandered into the kitchen at work, and said, "Hey, like, uh—I've got some extra time and like, how about swapping some work now for some lunch later?"

She knew her way around the kitchen pretty well, and we hit it right off. Things were going great, we were rolling pizza dough when she said, "Hey, like let's do agar for dessert . . ."

I looked up, stunned—she had seemed like such a nice girl. I knew my time was up; no more excuses. "Okay, just exactly what is this stuff anyway?"

Later, of course, I couldn't believe I'd gone for so long without taking advantage of this amazing food. It's a perfect natural gelatin—tasteless, dissolves completely and quickly, and some companies have started packaging it in flakes instead of bars for easy measuring.

1 jar (4 cups) Lakewood Peaches and Cream or Lakewood Strawberries and Cream *(If you have never seen this at your store, then ask for it. It's pretty easily available and very good. It makes the best desserts, and it's made with coconut milk, not cow's milk. You would never believe it because it's so rich.)*

2 bars agar-agar, or 1 cup agar flakes *(Read the label to make sure of your proportions.)*

1 teaspoon vanilla

1 cup sliced peaches or strawberries *(according to whichever juice you're using)*

Pour the juice into a saucepan, and let it come to a slow boil. If you are using flakes, put them in. If you are using bars, run them under water until they are soft and just put them in the pot. Stir until dissolved. Turn down and simmer about 15 minutes. Add the vanilla and the sliced fruit, and cook until the fruit just starts to ooze its juices. Pour into custard dishes or a pie plate. Chill until firm (about 2 hours).

Can you believe that's all there is to it? It really is so easy, and it tastes good. Once you've tried it, you won't be able to stop—ideas will pop into your head like crazy.

Tootie's Praline Cookies

Yield: 2 dozen

Excluding chocolate chip, these are the best cookies I have ever had. It's my grandmother's recipe and one that I still beg her to make when I take a trip home.

1 cup soy margarine
½ cup packed brown sugar
½ cup sugar
1 egg or egg replacer
1 teaspoon vanilla
2 cups unbleached flour
½ teaspoon baking soda
¼ teaspoon salt
½ cup finely chopped pecans

Brown sugar frosting:
1 cup firmly packed brown sugar
½ cup half-and-half or soymilk
1 tablespoon soy margarine
1½ to 1⅔ cups powdered sugar

1 pecan half per cookie

Preheat the oven to 350°F. Beat the margarine at medium speed with an electric mixer, and gradually add the sugars, mixing well. Add the egg and vanilla. Combine the flour, soda, and salt, and add gradually to the creamed mixture. Stir in the pecans. Chill this dough for 30 minutes.

Make the frosting by combining the brown sugar and half-and-half in a saucepan. Cook over medium heat, stirring constantly, until the mixture comes to a boil. Simmer for 4 minutes, remove from the heat, and stir in the margarine. Add enough powdered sugar to make the spreading consistency you want.

Roll the chilled dough with your hands into 1-inch balls, place on an ungreased cookie sheet, and bake for 10 to 12 minutes. Cool on racks. Spread with the brown sugar frosting, and top each cookie with a pecan half.

Mini-Ha-Ha Cake

Yield: 10 to 12 servings

1¼ to 1½ cups applesauce (or a slightly
    smaller amount of apple juice)
¾ cup oats
1½ cups white flour
2 teaspoons baking soda
½ cup soy margarine
½ to ¾ cup honey (You could also use any
    mixture of molasses, brown sugar, or
    malt.)
1 egg or egg replacer
1 teaspoon vanilla
1 teaspoon cinnamon
½ teaspoon ginger

Heat the applesauce or juice, and pour over the oats. Let sit about 15 minutes.

Preheat the oven to 375°F. Mix the flour and soda together. Cream the margarine, honey, egg, vanilla, and spices. Stir in the applesauce and oats, then the flour mixture. Pour into a greased pie plate, and bake for about 40 minutes, or until a straw or toothpick comes out clean. Let it cool a bit and add the icing. (It's the icing that makes this a mini-ha-ha cake).

Mini-Ha-Ha Frosting

Yield: 4½ cups

1 cup water
2 cups brown sugar, or 1 cup brown sugar
    plus 1 cup honey
2 eggs or egg replacer
1½ teaspoons vanilla
Pinch of cream of tartar
¾ cup chopped raisins
¾ cup chopped toasted nuts

Over medium to medium-high heat, simmer the water and sweetener until it comes off a lifted spoon in a line about the size of a thread. Very quickly stir in the egg, vanilla, and cream of tartar. When smooth, add the chopped nuts and raisins, and spread on top of the cake.

The icing is good on almost any kind of cake, but I like it on this apple cake the best.

Chocolate Almond Cookies

Yield: 28 to 36 small cookies

To me, nothing tastes better together than choco-late and toasted almonds. I haven't had Swiss chocolate almond ice cream in years, and hope-fully I have put an end to my addiction to Hershey's chocolate almond bars. What's a girl to do?

One afternoon in a chocolate panic, I invented these cookies; they truly hit the spot.

1 cup oats
½ cup whole wheat flour
½ cup unbleached white flour
1 teaspoon baking powder
½ teaspoon baking soda
½ teaspoon salt
3 to 4 heaping tablespoons cocoa or carob powder
½ cup soy margarine
¾ cup molasses plus enough brown sugar to make 1 cup *(Just leave the molasses in the measuring cup, and add enough brown sugar to loosely make 1 uneven cup.)*
1 egg or egg replacer
1 teaspoon vanilla
1 cup toasted almonds,* cut coarsely into big chunks

*If your almonds aren't toasted, pop them into the oven while it's preheating. They can roast while you are mixing the other ingredients.

Preheat the oven to 350°F. Mix the dry ingredients into a medium-sized bowl. Cream the margarine, molasses and sugar, egg, and vanilla either by hand or with a mixer until smooth. Add the dry ingredients to the creamed mixture, mix well, and stir in the nuts. Drop small- to medium-sized spoonfuls onto a greased cookie sheet, and bake about 10 minutes. Let cool enough so that they do not instantly burn your tongue off, and enjoy immediately. They are serious winners!

Gingerbread

Yield: 10 to 12 servings

At heart, I'm a chocoholic. I'm making a serious effort to give up white sugar once and for all. In the meantime, when I need something so sweet that it makes my teeth hurt, I make gingerbread. This recipe is so great—no brown sugar, no honey, just one cup of molasses. As soon as fall comes and there's a little bite in the air, I'm subjected to a primal urge that forces me to leave work early, go home, and make gingerbread. God, the smell of it! And it's so easy. I like it hot right out of the oven, slathered in margarine. Steven eats his with a big piece of sweet potato pie; amazingly enough he calls this "a la mode." With applesauce it makes a great afternoon snack, or with hot lemon-honey sauce drizzled over the top it makes a killer midnight snack. This recipe is so easy. So what's stopping you?

1 cup whole wheat flour
½ cup oats
½ teaspoon baking soda
1 rounded tablespoon ground ginger
1 teaspoon cinnamon
¼ teaspoon allspice
½ cup soy margarine or vegetable oil
1 cup unsulfered molasses *(dark or light, not blackstrap)*
2 eggs or egg replacer
2 teaspoons vanilla
½ cup soymilk
1 big handful raisins
2 big handfuls chopped walnuts or pecans

This is one of the few recipes that I use an electric mixer on. If you have one, it works great; if you don't, mixing this by hand works just as well. Preheat the oven to 350°F. Mix the dry ingredients in a bowl. Cream the margarine or oil, molasses, eggs, vanilla, and soymilk. Add the dry ingredients and mix well. Add the raisins and nuts, and give another quick stir. Pour into an oiled 9 x 13-inch pan or a 9-inch glass pie plate, and bake for 35 to 40 minutes until a straw or toothpick stuck in the middle comes out clean. You may have to run a knife around the edges of the pan to get this out smoothly. Enjoy!

Rhubarb Cobbler

Yield: 6 to 8 servings

One of my father's favorite expressions is, "Do you think the rain will hurt the rhubarb?" As a girl I never knew what he meant. I was grown up before I realized it is just another way of saying, "What's going on?"

2 pounds diced fresh rhubarb
2¼ cups sugar
4 tablespoons plus 4 teaspoons soy
    margarine
Juice of 1 lemon
1 teaspoon salt
1 egg or egg replacer
1 tablespoon baking powder
1 cup flour
1 teaspoon cinnamon
1 tablespoon vanilla
½ cup buttermilk, or ½ cup soymilk
    plus 1 teaspoon vinegar

Preheat the oven to 375°F. In a saucepan, combine the rhubarb, 2 cups of the sugar, 4 tablespoons of the margarine, and the lemon juice. Stir and cook until a syrup starts to form and the rhubarb gets soft. It should take about 7 minutes. Remove from the heat.

Cream together the remaining margarine and sugar. (Use a mixer if you have one.) Add the egg, baking powder, flour, cinnamon, vanilla, and buttermilk. Mix until this looks like a cake batter. Pour the rhubarb into a 9 x 13-inch greased casserole dish. Pour the batter over the rhubarb, and bake about 35 minutes, or until the center is done. This is good with vanilla ice cream on top.

Carrot Cake

Yield: 8 to 10 servings

This is my favorite cake recipe. You never have to worry if it's light enough—it's going to be heavy, dark, dense, delicious, and just right!.

2 cups flour
2 teaspoons baking soda
½ teaspoon salt
2 teaspoons ground cinnamon
3 eggs or egg replacer
2 cups sugar
¾ cup canola or corn oil
¾ cup buttermilk, or ¾ cup soymilk
    plus 1 to 2 teaspoons vinegar
2 teaspoons vanilla extract
2 cups grated carrots
One 8-ounce can crushed pineapple
1 small can flaked coconut *(or grate your own)*
1 cup chopped pecans or walnuts

Preheat the oven to 350°F. Grease a 9 x 13-inch baking dish or three 9-inch cake pans (if you want to, but I never make anything that fancy).

Stir together the flour, baking soda, salt, and cinnamon. Beat the eggs, sugar, oil, milk, and vanilla with a mixer until smooth. Add the flour mixture and continue beating at low speed until blended. Gently fold in the carrots, pineapple, coconut, and nuts. Bake for 30 to 35 minutes until a straw or toothpick inserted in the middle comes out clean.

Cream "Cheese" Icing

¾ cup soy margarine
12 ounces soy cream cheese
    (1½ packages)
3 cups powdered sugar
2 teaspoons vanilla extract

Cream the margarine and cream cheese with a mixer or by hand. Add the powdered sugar and vanilla. Beat until smooth and spread on the carrot cake.

Molasses Cake

Yield: 10 servings

Why I see her now in the open door,
Where the little gourd grew up the sides,
*   and o'er*
The clapboard roof!—And her face—ah me!
Wasn't it good for a boy to see—
And wasn't it good for a boy to be
Out to Old Aunt Mary's.

The jelly—the jam and the marmalade,
And the cherry and quince "preserves"
*   she made!*
And the sweet-sour pickles of peach and pear,
With cinnamon in 'em, and all things rare!—
And the more we ate was the more to spare,
Out to Old Aunt Mary's

James Whitcomb Riley

The best part of this cake is the icing. It's good on
any spice cake or oatmeal cake. I'm bad about
leaning over the counter and picking the icing off
this cake bit by bit.

½ cup soy margarine
3 eggs or egg replacer
2 cups molasses
3 cups self-rising flour, or 3 cups
    unbleached flour, 1 tablespoon baking
    powder, and ¾ teaspoon salt

Preheat the oven to 325°F. Melt or soften the margarine to room temperature. Combine the margarine and eggs with the molasses until creamy. Add the flour or flour mixture, and combine until you have a smooth batter. Bake in a 9 x 13-inch shallow rectangle pan for 30 minutes.

Broiled Icing

Yield: 3½ cups

1 cup light brown sugar
¼ cup soy margarine
¼ cup milk or soymilk
1 cup chopped nuts
1 cup coconut

Mix all the ingredients well, and spread on the warm cake. Put the cake back in the oven, and broil for 2 to 3 minutes. Watch closely so it doesn't burn.

Picking Blackberries

Few can resist the lure of the blackberry, like the siren's song. Fewer can navigate the stickers. How many times have I found myself dangling over a twenty-foot cliff, covered with briars, stickers, and poison ivy, reaching for that one perfect berry just inches from my grasp? My father says picking blackberries is therapy. One day every June, he gets his friends to give up golf and go with him to pick berries. What a sight—bankers, stockbrokers, and CEOs, all vying for the perfect berry!

How many foods do you have to dress for in order to gather? To get blackberries at my house, I have to:

1. Get up very early;

2. Slather my whole body with Skin-So-Soft (the only bug repellent that works);

3. Dress in white or light-colored clothing (to repel the ticks);

4. Wear long-sleeved clothes. And long pants are a must for the stickers and briars (even though it's approximately 85 degrees at 6 o'clock in the morning and will be about 98 degrees before I'm done);

5. Keep one eye peeled for the snakes who love the berries too.

6. Wear a briar-proof glove on the left hand so I can pull away the briars and reach for the perfect berry.

Is it all worth it? YES! Eating a blackberry right off the cane is as close as you can come to eating a sundrop. What else could entice a biker to pull off the highway and fill his helmet with fresh berries. It is the Siren's Blackberry Call.

Blackberry Cake

Yield: 10 servings

This is a good alternative to cobbler, and if you freeze lots of berries, you can make this in winter for a special treat.

2 cups sugar
1 cup soy margarine
4 eggs or egg replacer
4¼ cups flour
1 teaspoon baking powder
1 teaspoon baking soda
1 cup buttermilk, or 1 cup soymilk plus
    1 teaspoon vinegar
1 teaspoon vanilla
2 cups fresh blackberries *(can be frozen but not sweetened)*

1 cup powdered sugar
Soymilk, as needed

Preheat the oven to 350°F. Cream the sugar and margarine. Add the eggs and blend again until very smooth. Mix the flour, baking powder, and baking soda, and combine the buttermilk and vanilla. Add dry and liquid ingredients alternately to the creamed mixture, and stir well after each addition. Fold in the berries. If you're using frozen berries, thaw and drain before adding.

Pour the batter into a greased and floured Bundt pan, and bake for 1¼ hours. Let cool at least 10 minutes, then invert the pan; the cake should slip out. Don't try to cut this cake until completely cool.

To make an icing, add soymilk to the powdered sugar, 1 tablespoon at a time, until it makes a consistency that will drizzle over the cake.

Peaches and Dumplings

Yield: 6 to 8 servings

My husband used to be a semi-truck driver. Occasionally, I would accompany him on his treks over the western slope of the Rocky Mountains. On one trip, we had to pick up peaches. (Yes, they really do grow peaches on the western slope of the Rocky Mountains.) Just getting to the peach farm was an adventure. It perched on the side on a mountain with roads made for small 4-wheel-drive vehicles, not semis. Somehow we made it to the peach farm, 9 wheels hanging off the road the whole way. When we got there, no peaches! Workers were all over the place picking as fast as they could go. The owner came running over, "Just give us a few more hours and we'll be done."

I sat in the truck for a while and then figured I might as well get in the groove. I got me a ladder and started picking. What an experience! I admit, I ate more peaches than I picked. I had peach juice running down my arms, dripping off my chin, sticking to my legs, and I didn't even care. I went into a kind of feeding frenzy—they were the best peaches I have ever had. It was all day before the peaches were ready, and really they were too ripe to be picked anyway, but what did I care, I had gone to Peach Heaven. In a way, that day ruined me for peaches. I hold every peach I eat now up to that same zenith, and none has ever compared. But that doesn't mean I won't stop trying!

This is a good old-fashioned way to indulge your peach craving. You may also substitute 2 cups berries for the peaches.

1 cup unbleached flour
1 cup sugar
1½ teaspoons baking powder
½ teaspoon baking soda
¼ teaspoon salt
1 egg or egg replacer
½ cup plus 2 tablespoons buttermilk,
    or ½ cup soymilk plus ½ teaspoon
    vinegar
1 tablespoon melted soy margarine
¼ teaspoon cinnamon
½ teaspoon ginger
5 cups sliced, peeled ripe peaches

Sift the flour, 2 teaspoons of the sugar, the baking powder, soda, and salt together. In a separate bowl, mix the egg, buttermilk, and soy margarine together. Quickly stir into the flour mixture, and barely combine. Set aside.

Pour 2 cups water into a non-aluminum saucepan. Add the remaining sugar, the cinnamon, and ginger, and bring to a boil. Add the peaches and simmer for 3 minutes. Do not overcook the fruit.

Drop the dumpling batter by spoonfuls into the simmering fruit. Cover and cook for 8 to 10 minutes until the dumplings are firm. Remember—no peeking while the dumplings are cooking. Serve with a big dollop of non-dairy ice cream.

Patsy's Own Peanut Butter Blossoms

Yield: 28 to 36 cookies

These may seem like the kind of cookies you can't make unless you're a grandmother, but they're Patsy's favorites and believe me, she's no grand-mother.

1¾ cups flour
½ teaspoon salt
1 teaspoon baking soda
½ cup soy margarine
¾ cup honey
½ cup peanut butter
1 egg or egg replacer
2 tablespoons soymilk or water
1 teaspoon vanilla
Chocolate or carob kisses

Preheat the oven to 350°F. Mix the flour, salt, and baking soda in a bowl. Cream the margarine, honey, and peanut butter in another bowl, and when smooth, add the egg, soymilk, and vanilla, and stir again until smooth. Stir in the dry ingredients. Roll walnut-size pieces of dough in the palms of your hands until you have round balls. Place on an ungreased cookie sheet, and bake about 8 minutes. Then remove from the oven and press a kiss into the middle of each ball until the edges crack a little. Bake about 4 minutes more.

Properly Made Tea

The best dessert is even better with a delicious cup of tea. You can't just dunk a tea bag in a mug of hot water and expect the same results as you would if you made a pot of tea just right. So here's some tips on how to do it:

1. Start with freshly drawn water. You don't have to go to the well, but don't use the same water that's been sitting on the stove all day.

2. Rinse out your teapot with very hot water to warm it up as well as clean it.

3. Go ahead and put the tea leaves in the pot. The heat from the pot will make the leaves begin to release their aroma.

4. When the water comes to a rolling boil, it's ready (not when it starts to bubble a little bit, and not when it's been boiling for 15 minutes). The longer water boils, the more oxygen it looses, and this makes it taste flat. Pour the water over the tea leaves, and cover the pot. Let steep for 3 to 5 minutes depending on how strong you like it. Some herb teas can brew up to 15 minutes without turning bitter. Black teas don't take nearly as long.

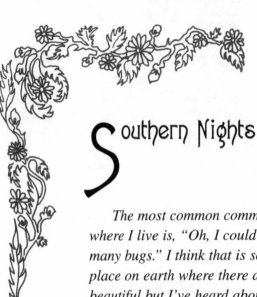

Southern Nights

The most common comment I get when someone finds out where I live is, "Oh, I could never live in the South, too many bugs." I think that is so funny. Bugs. As if there is a place on earth where there are no bugs. Maine, yes, it's beautiful but I've heard about those black flies. And New York City is high-falutin' but I've seen those roaches. They may have the "Lullaby of Broadway"—well, we have the "Lullaby of Bugway."

It's the sounds of the bugs that we Southerners love, the night sound. The Southern night has a sound all its own. Peepers and baby green frogs are always the first sign of spring, and then the lightning bugs, the enchanted lightning bugs, arrive, soon to be joined by the chirps of crickets, whirs of katy-dids, and the rhythmical sawing of the grasshoppers. Once summer is in full swing and all the frogs are out singing and croaking and rasping and growling and squeaking (one actually sounds like a crazy person laughing, really, the leopard frog), be ready for the buzz-buzz-buzz of the cicadas. Every once and awhile you hear a screech owl or the "who-cooks-for-you" hoot of the great horned owl, or

the shriek of a raccoon. The drip of dew off a tree branch onto the tin roof keeps rhythm with the carpenter frogs, and the chorus frogs start up just about then.

One night we had dinner and watched the "Three Tenors" give a special performance on PBS. Later, as we sat on the porch enjoying a starry night, our neighbor's cows seemed to be mooing very loudly and more often than usual. Soon Pinkie, our pet blind bull, joined in. Those cows were reaching notes the tenors just dream about. Far away you could hear a rooster crow, a dog bark; farther away, you could hear teen-agers drag racing. Along with all the other sounds, it seemed the whole night was serenading us—beating to some raw animal beat, pulsing all 'round us.

This is just the reason I don't have air conditioning—sleeping all night with the windows open is a luxury I could never give up. The sounds are all too magical, too good of a reminder when you wake in the night and wonder why you are alive, that what we are all doing—the bugs, the frogs, the birds, the animals, the trees, the stars, the breeze, the night—is just breathing.

Household Hints

1. Leave tomatoes in the window a couple of days before you eat them. This really helps store-bought tomatoes and takes away the mealy taste.

2. To ripen an avocado, wrap it in a brown paper bag and put it on top of the refrigerator for a few days.

3. Do you know how to care for cast-iron? First of all, you can get beautiful pieces at most hardware stores or army surplus. The new ones need to be seasoned just like the old ones you might buy used. They will take a little more elbow grease just to make sure they are clean.

   First, scrub it good with steel wool and soap; even old rusty pans will clean right up. This is the ONLY time you should ever use soap on your cast-iron. Rinse it well and dry it off. Cover the whole thing, top, bottom, and handle, with a generous coating of oil. Put it in a 100°F oven for at least the whole day. Some people say you can do this for a week. I always pick a good cold day when I don't mind having the oven on all day. Use strictly for frying and sautéing for a while, not steaming or boiling.

About everyday cleaning: Wiping with a paper towel should be more than sufficient. If you feel like it needs a little bit more of a cleaning, just use a nylon scrubbie, hot water, and some elbow grease; NO SOAP! Always dry your cast-iron immediately. Put on a burner over low heat, and brush with a little oil when dry (if needed). This will help keep your skillet seasoned. Don't ever store leftovers in cast-iron! Never put it in the dishwasher!

If you get a piece of cast-iron that is old and rusty, but still beautiful, have a bonfire! That's the best way to get your cast-iron back to ground-zero. Literally, put it right in the middle of the fire, and let it glow red. Dig it out the next day, and it'll be ready for scrubbing and seasoning.

These seasoning instructions are the same for breaking in a wok. Another way of seasoning a wok is to make a lot of popcorn in it. Cleaning, drying, and caring information is also the same.

4. To wash greens or lettuce: Granny said this is what her mother always told her, "Wash them until you are sure there is not one speck of grit, and then wash them one more time."

5. If iced tea has gone cloudy from sitting in the refrigerator, add a splash of boiling water to clear it up.

6. To peel tomatoes quickly for sauce or canning: Fill a medium-size saucepan with water, and let it come to a gentle simmer. With a slotted spoon, gently place a few tomatoes at a time in water, leaving each one in about 1 minute. Remove with the slotted spoon, and rinse under cold water. The peel should slip right off.

7. When using soymilk or rice milk, there are sweetened ones and plain ones. Remember to read the label carefully before using. If you put the sweet kind in gravy, it will be dessert gravy and taste awful. It's great to use sweetened soymilk in dessert-style baked goods, but if you put it in something savory, you'll spoil it.

8. When making any salad that calls for hot ingredients being mixed with some kind of dressing (potato salad, pasta salad, copper pennies, lentil salad), be sure to add the ingredients when they are hot, as opposed to "Oh, I'll cook these potatoes now, put them in the refrigerator, go to the soccer game, come back, and make the salad." Mixing the ingredients when hot helps to marry the flavors and greatly improves the taste.

9. *I hope you love birds too. It is economical. It saves going to Heaven.*
   —Emily Dickinson

10. Sarah, my grandmother, always said, "Don't worry if something falls apart. That's how you know it will taste good." I have found this to be very good advice.

Index

186

187

Purchase these American ethnic and classic vegetarian cookbooks from your local bookstore or natural foods store, or you can buy them directly from:

Book Publishing Company
P.O. Box 99
Summertown, TN 38483
1-800-695-2241

Please include $3.50 per book
for shipping and handling

Flavors of the Southwest -
$12.95

Good Time Eatin' in Cajun Country - $9.95

Chili! - $12.95

Tofu Cookery - $15.95

New Farm Vegetarian Cookbook - $9.95